# The Bullhead Queen

To Toni —
Enjoy the Queen!
Sue

# The Bullhead Queen

## A YEAR ON PIONEER LAKE

### Sue Leaf

University of Minnesota Press

*Minneapolis*

*London*

Published by the University of Minnesota Press
111 Third Avenue South, Suite 290
Minneapolis, MN 55401-2520
http://www.upress.umn.edu

Library of Congress Cataloging-in-Publication Data

Leaf, Sue, 1953-
    The bullhead queen : a year on Pioneer lake / Sue Leaf.
        p. cm.
    ISBN 978-0-8166-6551-8 (hc : alk. paper) — ISBN 978-0-8166-6552-5 (pb : alk. paper)
    1. Human ecology—Minnesota—Chisago County. 2. Nature—Effect of human beings on—Minnesota—Chisago County. 3. Natural history—Minnesota—Chisago County. 4. Chisago County (Minn.)—History. 5. Chisago County (Minn.)—Environmental conditions. 6. Chisago County (Minn.)—Social life and customs. I. Title.
GF504.M6L43 2009
508.776'61—dc22

                                        2009015021

Printed in the United States of America on acid-free paper

The University of Minnesota is an equal-opportunity educator and employer.

18 17 16 15 14 13 12 11 10 09          10 9 8 7 6 5 4 3 2 1

# Contents

# Preface

Looking through my window past a fringe of green leaves, I can see Pioneer Lake sparkling in the morning sun. It is cool at the end of August, and the little lake is giving up its summer heat in wisps of fog curling from its surface. The patch of woods lining our shoreline is quiet, although I know that if I were to go looking, I would find small, nondescript birds skulking through the branches, birds that are already on migration.

Wild cherry and sumac, nonnative buckthorn and honeysuckle, dying elms and thriving ash trees all line the sloping path to the lake. It is a mixed forest with species from both its natural past and its human habitation.

On the northern end of the lake is a densely vegetated alder thicket arising from a substrate that is neither water nor soil, so it remains undisturbed by people. Here is the lake's last wild refuge, where one can find violet fleur-de-lis and dusty pink joe-pye weed, rosy swamp milkweed and spotted touch-me-not. Small birds nest in the brush of the alders and muskrats penetrate the watery interior.

On the southern shore, the imposing profile of Chisago Lake Lutheran Church dominates the horizon. Constructed of distinctive yellow brick by immigrant Swedes, and studded with bejeweled stained glass windows, the structure is of classic proportions, a landmark in Chisago County that draws admirers to its hand-carved interior from as far away as Europe.

The immigrant Swedes were not the first people on the lake, of course, but they are the pioneers that the name commemorates. The small, shallow body of water was a cattail bay of North Center Lake when the Swedes arrived in 1854. It was isolated from North Center and the other large Chisago Lakes—which the native Ojibwe referred to as one entity, "Kitchi-saga"—decades before my time here. A causeway was constructed that blocked its flow and dammed the bay, causing the water to pool. The lake that formed is seventy-seven acres, about the same size as another literary body of water, Walden Pond. Both are glacial in origin, and neither is an isolated, wilderness lake. Each is adjacent to human settlement, and each bears the mark of people.

But there the similarity ends. Where Walden Pond is deep and clear, Pioneer Lake is at most eight feet and not crystalline. Henry David Thoreau caught pike and pickerel on Walden; we catch only brown, slippery bullheads. Pioneer is, in truth, a bullhead queen, where the smooth, be-whiskered bottom feeders dwell in abundance.

However, despite the heavy hand of human beings that has changed Pioneer's nature, the little lake still exudes the unfettered exuberance of life. At certain times of the year, when the wind is up and sunlight glints off its surface, it appears wild, a northern lake. Wood ducks and Canada geese nest in its secret places, otters and red fox make use of hidden spaces. Migrating waterfowl rest on its waters, refueling on the bullheads that swim beneath.

In my thirteen years spent living on Pioneer, I have come to see how both north and south shores influence my life. I am formally trained to see what inhabits the alder thicket. Attracted by a magnetism that seems to pulse in my veins, I peer at its colorful, intricate denizens through my binoculars. I cannot resist their allure. But even as I stare into the tangle of branches and leaves, I am acutely aware of what lies to my back, the substantial structure of the church, and the theology of my childhood that so colors my relationship to nature. Are the residents of the alder thicket truly my brothers and sisters? What is my responsibility toward them? How far can I enter their world? What must I do to protect it?

I am a habitué of both the north and the south, and as such I mark the passage of time in two ways. I witness the turn of nature's seasons, the budding of trees, the leaves and the flowers, the loss of the chlorophyll, the dormant twigs. Spring, summer, fall, winter, the breathing in and breathing out of the natural year. At the same time, I observe the rotation of the church year, with its movement from Advent to Christmas to Lent, periods of celebration alternating with somber reflection. The two calendars are nicely meshed. There was enough of the Druid in the early church to ensure its anchorage in the natural world.

Pioneer Lake's water laps between these two shores, the north and the south, nature and religion. It is untouched and touched by human beings, wild but fettered. While I view it consciously as a biological entity, an ecosystem, I also perceive it in light of the assumptions I have been handed by Christianity: that I am free to tend it as I see fit, to groom its shoreline, eliminate its less desirable inhabitants, and change in subtle ways the composition of its waters.

Pioneer is aptly named as a somewhat man-made entity, emblematic of a new world, where human-induced climate change creates a new kind of nature, one more influenced by people than by glaciers, people who have acted on the assumptions of its church-dominated south shore. Yet we who would revel in and draw strength from nature, even a nature where the climate is shifting, retain the old ways of perceiving earth's creatures, the plants and animals of its waters and dry land. These old perceptions may no longer serve us well, may no longer be true—if, in fact, they ever were.

These essays, which open in Advent, the traditional time of entry, explore the north and south shores of Pioneer Lake. They are, like the lake, pioneers of the new world.

# Acknowledgments

The writing of any book takes place within a community whose members provide support and, often, food for thought, and so I thank my community, especially the members of Chisago Lake Lutheran Church and of Wild River Audubon, for helping me write these essays. I learn from you.

Matt Wikelius lent his expertise on trapping. Rollie Westman introduced me to the idea of "green burials." Anne Thom shared her ideas on lake associations and on multiple, conflicting uses of a small lake. Jim Huot-Vickery graciously agreed to read and comment on the final draft of the manuscript. Tom Anderson, Darby Nelson, and Doug Owens-Pike read and commented on early versions of some of the essays. And I want to recognize Tim Boettner, Andy Leaf, Jon Mansk, and Steve Schreiber, anglers extraordinaire, as the first to show obeisance to the Bullhead Queen.

The literary group Writersrisingup holds the annual Paul Gruchow Memorial Essay Contest and provided the opportunity for my work to be more widely read. I am grateful for its diligence in promoting writing on the most fundamental relationship of human beings—their link to nature.

I am fortunate to belong to a writing group that meets faithfully to critique each other's work. These wonderful writers have read nearly every essay in this book and provided invaluable critique. Past and present members include

Caren Stelson, Pam Schmid, Susan Narayan, Tara McAdams, Patti Isaacs, Judy Helgen, and Andrea Bolger. They are the midwives who helped birth *The Bullhead Queen*.

My children, Andy, Katie, John, and Christina Leaf, have been lead characters in some of the essays. My thanks to them for allowing me to pluck stories from their growing-up years.

Finally, my husband, Tom Leaf, read all the essays "hot off the pen" and became my most fervent cheerleader and truest believer in the heart of these essays. They live because he thought they were valuable. My love and my gratitude to him.

# Waiting at Advent

At the start of a new church year, we wait. The first season of the new year, Advent, means "to enter." We wait for Christmas, for the coming of the Child. A series of blue candles marks the progression of our patience: four candles, four Sundays until Christmas. But on the shores of Pioneer Lake, our household is waiting for something more tangible: ice. We anticipate the day when the lake will solidify and assume the dull sheen of polished metal.

Our family loves winter. My husband and I were introduced as children to winter sports that we thoroughly enjoy. Ice skating, tobogganing, cross-country skiing—once cold weather settles in, we live our days for the hours we spend on the ice, on the slopes, on the trail, drinking in the cold air and the stark beauty of snow and ice. For me, nothing marks the start of this beloved season as clearly as the ice-over of Pioneer Lake. So, in Advent, we are also waiting for winter.

Lakes in Minnesota have frozen every single winter of my life, and I have very few memories of impatience for ice to form. In my childhood, the nearest lake was a half-mile away. I couldn't keep a close watch, as I do now. But today, living on Pioneer, I am intimately involved in the day-to-day life of a lake. My interest in ice now has overtones: it takes but a minute to pick up my skates, walk down the path to the shore, sit on the dock, and lace up. The opportunity to be on the ice and to experience the pure joy of sailing across its gleaming surface could be mine every day.

Sadly, circumstances have changed. A friend at church, now in her seventies, tells me that, as a child, checking the ice for adequate thickness was a cherished routine after Thanksgiving dinner. Her father never let her venture out on new ice until at least that day, but often she and her siblings went skating after the turkey dinner, or within days. We no longer use Thanksgiving as a marker of when to expect ice on Pioneer. Several of the past thirteen autumns we have lived on the lake have been so warm that we have sometimes wondered if we'd get ice for Christmas. In these years, as climate change worsens, our winters come later and leave earlier. In North America, snow cover has decreased by several weeks on each end of the season.

This year, I hoped it might be different—normal, if you will, if my 1960s childhood could be the yardstick of normality. In mid-November, after a very warm fall, a howling cold front dropped the temperatures to nearly zero degrees one night. The next morning, Pioneer was strangely still, wrapped in that silence that materializes immediately upon ice-over, when the lap of waves has vanished. "Just like that!" I exulted in my journal that day. "So easy—ice before Thanksgiving!"

But I had neglected to see a small open circle out on the water in which dozens of Canada geese had taken refuge. The constant paddle of scores of webbed feet had kept ice from forming, and within days a northwest wind had gnawed open a large expanse of water and blown the shards to the far southern shore. Pioneer Lake was back to square one, but at least we observers knew now that the water temperature was very close to thirty-two degrees.

Reading through the journals I have kept of our years

on Pioneer, I find that the tendency for the lake to freeze, then open, and refreeze is common. Sometimes ice establishes itself overnight, in a sudden plunge of temperature; sometimes it forms with a slow sashay into immobility over several days and nights. Often, I have fretted that it froze with a wind, so that waves have been captured in its surface. (How does *that* happen?) Frequently, snow follows on the heels of ice-over, and I am unhappy that we won't be able to use the entire lake as a skating surface. It is a rare and glorious feeling to skate for miles on bare ice. Snow cover confines skaters to a rink, which we laboriously shovel to keep clear.

This year, since that cold spell, we have had rain and snow and a series of subfreezing nights. A snow at Thanksgiving left a continuous white blanket across the lake's surface, a reliable sign of an ice cover. We were disappointed to see wet cracks appearing soon after, indicating that what ice was present remained vulnerable to seepage from the dark water beneath it.

How unsettling it is to be unsure about Nature! Three weeks ago, I was not certain that Pioneer would freeze this winter. Indeed, there was a whisper in the Minneapolis *Star-Tribune* that some Minnesota lakes might remain open this year. I feel like I am continually holding a metaphorical hand to the planet's forehead—how feverish are you this year, Mother Earth? We—those of us in our technological societies who even think about such matters—are the first human beings in the history of our race to worry about earth's climate. People lived at the time of the glaciers, of course, but the great ice sheets came on slowly, over hundreds and even thousands of years. The subtle changes they brought over the course of a human lifetime might have been something grandparents could have told their grandchildren—should a rare early human being have lived to an unusually ripe old age to have grandchildren.

The fact that I worry would indicate my hope that, if we humans took action, we might actually change the course on which earth now seems set. Having loaded the atmosphere with all that carbon dioxide, it would seem to be our task to get rid of it—and keep the planet on an even keel. But I really wonder if even technological man has that kind of planetary control. Yes, we've set climate change in motion, but now that the tiger is out of the cage, why would we think it is merely a matter of coaxing it back in? Perhaps the big cat is really, truly wild and already beyond our control. What will my grandchildren do with the tiger?

This morning after breakfast, after I had blown out the one lit Advent candle, the dog and I trudged down to the water's edge as a fine mist fell. In early December, as we make preparations for Christmas, we are still waiting for cold weather. The waning days hurtle us toward the winter solstice. It is the time of year least easy for me to deny the reality of a warming planet.

Pioneer exhibited an unusual visage, more reminiscent of March than of early winter. It had been raining and water shimmered over a thin layer of ice. Close in, I could see cloudy patches where the water had frozen with air mixed in. In other areas, the clarity of the ice revealed the bottom sediments with bits of green aquatic plants scattered about. Pioneer's water is always clearest just before ice-over. I was less inclined to cheer this ice, having been fooled once. And surely, with vast puddles spread over the surface, the ice would be rough and uninviting to skaters, even if it suddenly turned colder.

A flock of geese silhouetted against the sullen morning sky appeared in the north. They circled and seemed to be landing. "So," I thought, "there is water out there somewhere." However, each bird glided on to a solid surface, not water, and settled into an upright stance, craning its neck and rearranging its wings. They seemed as surprised as I that the ice could hold their weight.

# Counting at Christmas

The snow is blinding, a white curtain veiling the world, as we make our way into the church narthex on a Saturday morning in mid-December. Singly and in pairs, members of Wild River Audubon arrive, stomping the snow off their boots, shaking scarves, and pounding their gloves. The night has delivered five inches of heavy snow, and it is not letting up. We are filled with delight.

People have gathered for the annual Christmas Bird Count, an event I eagerly anticipate. Our chapter always holds its count in the week before Christmas, which means that I will snatch time from the most hectic season of the year to participate. I do this deliberately—most of the folks gathered here do. We all have called a time-out to the holiday madness of shopping malls, spitting cash registers, and congestion in the Camel Lot. Marked by the act of slinging a pair of binoculars around our necks, we have said, "Just for today, we are going to appreciate a beautiful world."

In the gray, predawn light, Andy, the organizer for our chapter's count, hands out "rare bird sighting" forms, checklists, and county maps. Then we discuss territory assignments.

Our chapter's count is part of a greater event, National Audubon's Christmas Bird Count, an endeavor that has taken place annually since 1900. From coast to coast, fifty thousand Audubon members spend one day in the field counting birds, all the counts taking place in the ten days either side of Christmas. It is the longest-running, volunteer-based bird census in the world, and it provides valuable information on the long-term health of bird populations. Count data can be used to detect declining bird numbers, if a population is in trouble, or, in the opposite case, increasing. They can even be used to suggest the effects of climate change. For example, Duluth Audubon's count now regularly records cardinals, where they didn't twenty years ago.

Each chapter has a count circle fifteen miles in diameter, so the area of a count is the same, year after year. Our circle's epicenter is about three miles north of the church at the intersection of two county roads. From there, Andy outlines portions of the circle and assigns them to teams of counters. Teams like to specialize in a particular wedge of circle year after year. We get to know the hot spots that harbor birds, and we establish a routine with the residents. They come to expect us each year and often greet us with hot drinks and Christmas treats.

Again this year, Andy assigns my husband, Tom, and me to the northeastern wedge of the circle. It's a portion of Chisago County that is still fairly rural, with some working dairy farms, many hobby farms, the New England–like village of Taylors Falls, and the federally protected St. Croix River, bordering Wisconsin. We will not count birds on the river, however. That portion of the wedge will be covered by Dorothy and Mike, a couple with more seniority.

There's an unofficial ranking to how the areas are assigned. Although Tom and I have been counting for ten years, we're relative newcomers. We were originally assigned our wedge because it hadn't had regular counters before. While it might seem an idyllic territory, rural with lots of open space, it usually lacks something essential: open water.

In winter, birds cluster around open water. The chance of seeing an unusual bird by a bubbling creek is much higher than in a broad expanse of woods or field. In our wedge, the St. Croix will still be open in mid-December, but the many small marshes and ponds will be capped with ice.

We actually like our count area. We like the challenge of developing our eagle eyes to seek out uncommon birds. "They're out there," we tell ourselves. "We've just got to find them." We also know more than half the people owning the farms and yards we'll visit. Because Pioneer Lake is only a mile south of our wedge, these people are our neighbors, and most attend the yellow brick church where we've gathered this morning. Each year, several weeks before the count, we buttonhole them after service and tell them: get your feeder ready! Keep it stocked with seed! Have you thought about offering peanut butter? Suet? Cracked corn? Try it to see what you'll draw in! It's nice public relations for Audubon, and it connects people to nature, one of our chapter's aims.

Having agreed on what portion we'll cover, Tom and I don our layers—sweater, polar fleece, wind shell, scarf, and hat—and prepare to head out. It's not that cold out, only about twenty degrees, but bird watching is not a vigorous activity, and we stand about in the wind, staring at bird feeders. It's nice to be warmly dressed.

In the fifteen minutes we were inside, the car has become cloaked in snow, and we brush off the windshield and back window before getting in, slamming the doors good to loosen snow clinging to the sides. We have never had so much snow on a bird count. Tom noses the car out of the parking lot and heads north. The plows have swiped only once down the county roads, and I'm glad he's driving. We could get stuck if the car wanders out of the packed-down ruts in the road.

The first stop each year is at Glenn and Elsie Reed's. They are retired farmers who have built a new house across the road from their farm, which their son now works. Glenn's a deer hunter, and if he gets his deer in the fall (he usually does), he'll hang the rib cage up from a tree limb in his back-yard. It sounds and looks barbaric—but it's a common prac-tice, and the birds love it.

It is 8:00 A.M. when we ease our way into the Reeds' snowy driveway. There's the rib cage, rotating in the wind at the edge of the woods, a black-and-white hairy wood-pecker perched on the sternum, eating breakfast. Tom and I pause a moment inside the car to survey the busy feeder nearby. It's a clever structure, designed to look like a stop-light, with feeding ports where the green, yellow, and red lights should be. Chickadees and nuthatches fly back and forth, taking one sunflower seed with each visit and crack-ing it open on a perch close at hand.

"I see three, no four chickadees," I murmur, looking through my binoculars.

"Five, six," Tom counts, as two more fly in.

"There's a red-bellied woodpecker on that oak," I point out, and then start a list, our data sheet for the day. We'll record each species and how many individuals of each spe-cies we see.

Glenn and Elsie are up and dressed, and invite us in to the warmth of their entry porch. We take them up on the offer, but we don't linger. The sun is up now (not that we can actually see it through the snow) and the day is bright-ening. Birds will be most active early, restocking their small bodies with calories after burning them off through the long, cold night.

Leaving the Reeds, we pass the Taggatz place. It used to be one of our most fruitful stops, with an active feeder, corncobs strapped to tree limbs for squirrels, and a large crab apple, laden with withering pippins that attracted waxwings and stray robins. But Harold, the elderly man who kept the feeder stocked, has passed on and now lies in Hillside Cemetery. The year after his death, we drove into the farmyard, only to find an empty feeder. Indeed, the place resembled Sleeping Beauty's castle, with brambles already wrapping around the low-standing platform feeders that had been placed to attract pheasants and cardinals. Even the unpruned crab apple looked brushy.

On a whim, we back up and drive into the old Taggatz place. It's been several years since our last visit, and the feeders are entirely gone. The old farmhouse sags and badly needs a paint job, and a new, modest rambler sits a ways off at the edge of the farmyard. Still, we scare up a small flock of tree sparrows, foraging in the goldenrod. As we turn around and get ready to leave, a woman in a housecoat comes out of the new home and runs up to the car. She's got a question for us. In November, she saw three big birds, a family, she thought. They were huge, maybe six feet tall, grayish-brown with red caps and long legs. They had been eating something in the field north of the house.

Her description is dead-on. "Sandhill cranes," we tell her, without hesitation, as Tom grabs the National Geographic guide and locates a picture of the gangly birds.

"That's it! That's what I saw. Will they come back?" she wonders.

"They might have been migrating," we tell her, "but we know they nest around here. You may get lucky and have them return to nest next spring." We are tickled to be able to answer her question and note her interest. A good-bye wave and we head back to the main road.

A half-mile past Taggatzes' we turn on a gravel road to visit Chris and Karl Ruser's farm. We look for, and usually find, American tree sparrows in the hedgerow lining their driveway. Today, however, I notice a flutter of many small wings in an abandoned pasture south of the farm, and Tom slams on the brakes. I pop out of the car and scan the field with the binocs. Dozens of tree sparrows. Dozens! We count seventy-one—okay, it's an estimate—and continue on to Rusers', where there are zero. Chris, however, points out pigeons—rock pigeon is the official label—perched on the silo.

Chris was a Minnesota farm girl when she met and fell in love with Karl, a New Jersey boy who had ventured into the Midwest for college. They now farm an unusual crop: native prairie plants. They have small test plots here and there, stands of prairie grasses that are harvested for seed, and seasonal greenhouses that nurture young seedlings in the spring. We always eyeball the prairie patches to see if any birds are holed up in them but come up empty today.

Our next stop is Edna Goranson's place. Edna is in her nineties and still active. She lives by herself in the small, tidy farmhouse where she raised her family. Her daughters live nearby, and a cousin and her daughter down the road. All the women live on land once owned and farmed by a common ancestor, their grandfather, a Swedish immigrant. Edna tends a little platform feeder that for some reason attracts many cardinals.

Edna has been waiting for us.

"Oh, come in, come in," she says warmly, a trace of Swedish lilt lingering in her speech. "I have been seeing my cardinals this morning!"

The coffeepot is perking on the stove, and there is a dazzling array of Christmas cookies laid on a pretty plate on the kitchen table. The Swedes have an unwritten rule about serving seven different types of cookies with company coffee, a rule Tom's grandmother scrupulously observed, so we're acquainted with this protocol. An Advent wreath next to the cookies is aflame with all four candles lit. It is that close to Christmas.

We stand by the window over the kitchen sink and count what we see at the feeder—business first—then accept steaming mugs of coffee and start in on the cookies. Edna has a girlish laugh and pretty blue eyes, and she's interested in how the morning has gone, with all the snow. She cautions us not to get stuck when we leave, but we're not worried—yet. Edna's driveway and the gravel road leading to it are fairly flat.

Onward.

We wind in and out of side roads off the main county road that forms the southernmost edge of our part of the count. The snow swirls about. It is a very white world—sky and fields, all variations on the snow's pure hue. The mild temperature is a boon for watching birds. Knitted gloves suffice to keep our hands warm when we're out of the car using binoculars. There have been some counts when we've really needed mittens and our hands numbed quickly, making it hard to manipulate the focus wheel on the field glasses.

By late morning, we're at our halfway point in Taylors Falls and stop at Coffee Talk for more caffeine and their celebrated bear claws, a buttery pastry with almond paste. Our stomachs have been rumbling for more than an hour. The little coffeehouse is fragrant with the aroma of ground coffee beans. Christmas lights strung along the windows cast a warm glow over the room and carols jingle out of a PA system. Just for a moment I am pulled back into the world of holiday lists: we still haven't put up our tree! I need to bake some spritz for the carol sing tomorrow at church! And shouldn't we get one more present for Tim?

No, not now, I remind myself. Instead, Tom and I review our bird tally so far. Why haven't we seen any house finches yet? What are the chances we'll see a bald eagle out by Wild Mountain? Remember the harrier we saw in that field above the bluff?

It is not accidental that the bird count falls in the most frantic season of the year. The event was proposed in 1900 as an alternative to the tradition of a Christmas bird shoot, in which revelers went into the woods to shoot anything with feathers. Some say that the shoot has its origins in Druid custom. Druids considered the wren prophetic. A captured wren could foretell what the coming new year would bring. Over time, the Druid connection was lost, but the hunt continued, taking place on the day after Christmas, Saint Stephen's Day, the day that the Church observes the event of the slaughter of the Holy Innocents.

In this day and age it is hard to imagine such a reckless disregard for wildlife, particularly songbirds. I'm pleased to be part of a long line of crusaders advocating peaceable coexistence with nature. With this final thought, Tom and I pull on our hats and return the coffee mugs to the dirty dishes bin.

We head north out of town along the St. Croix, which flows dark and forceful past lacy ledges of ice. We know we're not supposed to count the waterfowl on the river (that's Dorothy and Mike's area), but at a point in the road where it is an easy hike to the water's edge, we pause and walk out for a look-see. There are a hundred Canada geese at rest in a backwater, honking softly to themselves. Interspersed among their gray forms are white trumpeter swans. Some of the swans have dark bands—artificial tracking collars—around their necks.

Trumpeter swans are an endangered species, and on most Christmas Bird Counts in other areas the sight of them would cause counters to swoon. But not here; for more than a decade there has been a captive breeding program at Crex Meadows Wildlife Area in the upper St. Croix valley, where young swans are released each summer. They regularly find their way down river into our area, to stretches where the water remains open all winter, and flock with geese. We wonder if Dorothy and Mike will happen on this big flock. It's six miles out of Taylors Falls and not discernible from the bridge over the river. We think we'd better count them.

Scanning the group with my binocs, I detect movement on the opposite shore. Zeroing in, I see people standing near the river's edge, people in Wisconsin looking through binoculars at the geese. They're like our mirror image, and I'm amused, thinking of the unsuspecting birds being such a focus of human interest. Then, the observer I'm observing turns, and I catch a glint of red hair. Hey, wait a minute. It's Mike and Dorothy . . . in Wisconsin! They've gone over to the other side on our bird count. Is that legit?

At any rate, these aren't our birds. We relinquish them to their rightful counters and slog back through the snow to the car.

After leaving the St. Croix, our next stop is at a small spring-fed marsh on the southern edge of Wild River State Park that sometimes has open water. We hoped there might be a wayward teal or merganser there, but the water, dark against the fresh snow, is empty. Then, gazing through the gauzy curtain of snow that has eased slightly, we detect a dark form in an ash at the water's edge. A hawk! A buteo, we narrow it further, noting its relatively big head and short tail. It is most likely a red-tailed, by far the most common buteo in our area this time of year, but the light is poor. We can't see the red tail, or a bellyband, a swath of dark feathers across the lower breast.

Tom keeps an eye on the bird, who is seemingly unperturbed by our presence, while I go back to the car to retrieve the Sibley guide, the definitive source, to see what our options are. Rough-legged hawks are possible. So are red-shoulders, both buteos, like the red-tailed—cousins.

If we can't ID this bird, we can't include it in our tally. There is a certain cachet to being able to report unusual birds at the end of the day, when all counters come back together. "Ooh, a kingfisher!" other counters might say. "Where'd you see it?" Or, "A tufted titmouse? I don't believe it!" (For the record, we have not had tufted titmice on our Christmas Bird Count. Ever.) In any case, I want our hawk to not be a red-tail, but something less common.

I'm in luck. After fifteen minutes of being scrutinized, the hawk grows weary of the attention and takes off. As it glides overhead, I scan its dark form and catch sight of a pair of red shoulder patches, almost glowing in the weak afternoon light. A red-shouldered hawk, on the northernmost edge of its *summer* range. Oh, what a find!

The marsh borders a lovely mature sugar maple stand. The people who own it maintain a large, immensely attractive bird feeding station in their yard with many different types of feeders. There are long column types, platforms and fly-throughs, suet feeders and corncobs strapped to trees. There's even a heated dog dish, providing fresh water. Despite the inclement weather, birds flit to and from the station, in constant motion. This yard, bustling with avian activity, will be our last stop.

Fresh snow caps the fence posts in the garden, drapes the large limbs of an oak from which is suspended one of the feeders, cloaks the roofs of the outbuildings. The yard is a little oasis for birds and people alike. The owners step outside the house for a moment to tell us they've seen four different woodpeckers that day—pileated, red-bellied, hairy, and downy. We can add all to our tally.

Our route is nearing its end. It is now midafternoon and the snow has tapered off. We turn our car, which never got stuck, toward home. We'll have just enough time to prepare a hotdish and tally birds at our own feeder before returning to church for a potluck.

The different groups will straggle in around five o'clock, in the early dark of the winter solstice. They will bear in their hands casseroles wrapped in thick towels, Tupperware containing salads, pans of bars covered by aluminum foil. After we eat, we will compile all the tallies: how many downy woodpeckers? Trumpeter swans? Mallards? We usually record about forty-two species, about six thousand individual birds. The most common bird seen is almost always a nonnative, the European starling. The most common native bird is one that many would like to be able to shoot, the American crow.

Our numbers are low, as far as bird counts go, reflecting a northern count in deforested farmland. By comparison, a count written up in *Audubon* magazine taking place in Mexico at the convergence of three richly diverse habitats recorded 158 species. But these are our birds, those forty-two species and this open, barren place our homeland. Nearly all of us have grown up with shorn farm fields, naked woodlots, and ice-capped marshes, and everyone would say we love the Zen-like quality of a simplified horizon in winter, a land bereft of leaves and color.

It seems appropriate to me that we absorb the simplicity of the winter landscape in these days before Christmas and incorporate it into our souls, so that we might probe the meaning of what we celebrate so frantically. The Christmas Bird Count gives us opportunity to do this and to live a few hours in its grace.

# Wild Ice

Christmas Eve. The phrase evokes images of glowing candlelight and glinting tree ornaments. In our household, the morning of Christmas Eve is marked by a storm of activity. Kids bustle about, bellowing for scissors and Scotch tape, and wondering who used up the reindeer wrapping paper. The house is filled with the scent of fresh balsam—the tree came into the house only days earlier.

In the kitchen, I preside over the beginnings of our Christmas Eve dinner. The fruity scent of ruby-red lingonberries melds with the yeasty fragrance of stollen, baking in the oven. I aim for the right mix of tradition and innovation in our holidays, so we can view the grand feast of the Incarnation, God in human form, with continuously new eyes.

It's a lot for one fragile human being to handle. Sometimes I need to decompress. After lunch, desperate for fresh air and a brief intermission, I take up my ice skates and make my way down the path to the lake. Skating is always coupled with Christmas in my mind. The very skates I hold in my mittened hand as I head out to the ice were a Christmas gift from my parents almost forty years ago.

The skates are battered. The aging leather is yellowed and cracked, and the tops, looking like shoes you'd need a buttonhook for, resemble something out of *Little Women*. But they are serviceable, and my body knows them intimately, much like it knows my bicycle and my canoe paddle. My old-fashioned skates are a part of me.

I learned how to skate only a few years after I learned how to walk. My mother, who spent her girlhood skating on the frozen Mississippi at Little Falls, taught me. We started right out on single blades, wasting no time with the double set of runners many beginners use. I leaned on her for support, where other neophytes might use a chair, shuffling forward as she glided backward, arms outstretched to hold me.

There were spills, of course. On one memorable winter afternoon, as I skated backward in tandem with Mother, I caught a blade in a small crack in the ice and fell away, smacking my head hard. Shortly after, the school nurse informed my parents that I was badly nearsighted and needed glasses immediately. Medicine has yet to record a case where a blow to the cranium induced myopia. Still, my mother labored guiltily for years under a nagging suspicion that our passion for the ice had ruined my eyes.

As a suburban child, I skated on outdoor rinks. Every elementary school in Roseville had two rinks and a warming house that were maintained, complete with an attendant, until late February. I may have learned to skate from my mother, but I honed my skill at the Lake Owasso rink, on the west shore of the lake itself, through countless rounds of Pom-Pom-Pull-Away.

When I was an early teen, skating at the local rink after supper was the hot thing to do. It was a place to meet your friends, watch the boys, and exercise a bit of independence. For weeks after Christmas, a girlfriend and I walked the half-mile to the rink in the dark after supper. We adorned our skates with jingle bells and homemade pom-poms. Our wool skating socks, sometimes embroidered with yarn, were marks of fashion. With the same skates I now use, I'd skate for two hours, until the lights shut off and the warming house closed. In those years, sexual tension was added to the complex pleasure of flying over glossy ice with ease and grace, in the exhilarating cold of winter. I was profoundly sad when, at the end of February, the ice softened and turned to slush.

I bring a mix of psychological baggage to the ice this afternoon of Christmas Eve. Overstimulated by last-minute preparations, I seek the physical release that the ice will give me. I anticipate the pleasing repetition of steady strokes of the blades.

However, I am not prepared for sheer visceral thrill.

This is my first time skating this winter. Pioneer froze very late, only five days earlier. It finally iced over on a windless, subzero night. Very cold and very still: the recipe for excellent ice. From the shore the next morning, we saw the surface was like glass. A day later, a light snowfall cloaked the new ice. Not being able to see it, we were afraid to step onto it.

It is a shame that snow hid the ice from our eyes. It is always enlightening to gaze upon an oddity. Water is unique among liquids. Its molecules become farther apart, it becomes less dense, when it solidifies. As ice forms, the little $H_2O$ molecules arrange themselves into a crystalline lattice, with big pockets of space between them. For this reason, ice is lighter than water and floats. It is also why a lake expands while freezing and pushes against the metal supports of docks, sometimes bending them.

The Department of Natural Resources warns that four inches of ice are needed to support a person, but we know from experience that really only two inches will suffice. Once the lake freezes, we are on the ice as soon as humanly possible. (Yes, we have been stopped by the Chisago County sheriff.) If snow falls, and drifts form, it is hard to skate the full length, and it is really fun to go for miles and miles. Also, if temperatures rise, snow may fuse to the ice and ruin the gloss. Feeling this urgency to get on the ice has led us to skate when the ice bobbles up and down with every glide, when water oozes up through cracks, when we have observed open water just ahead, and abruptly turned around to head back to our boots on shore. This is part of the thrill.

Three days after ice-over, Tom edged out onto the ice and began to shovel. Each scrape revealed that the flawless ice had not been ruined by the snow. It was dark and clear: perfect. Cracks led him to gauge the thickness at one and one-half inches, so his decision to shovel was fairly gutsy—even more so since, a year before, he had done the very same thing and fallen through. The ice had given way with unnerving swiftness, with no warning, no preparatory cracking, as is seen in cartoons on TV. Tom simply dropped into waist-deep, numbing water, shovel in hand, a shocking experience.

But that didn't happen this time. Instead, being careful not to venture too far from shore, he shoveled a good-sized rink. There was a cracked seam, created by pressure from the ice, running across the surface. Tom noted that standing on one side of the seam depressed the surface so much that there was a half-inch difference between the two plates.

That was two days ago. I had been so caught up in holiday preparations I hadn't found time to skate. Now, as I sat on the disassembled dock and laced up (thinking of Jo March and of Amy, falling in) I could see that the ice was several inches thicker. At the shoreline, I surveyed the wintry scene. The lake was an expanse of new snow sparkling in the weak afternoon sunlight. Wispy, naked willows fringed the northern shore. To the south, on the hill with a commanding view of the lake, stood the yellow brick church, simple and elegant, cutting the blue sky. In less than an hour, I would join family, friends, and neighbors in the warmth of its sanctuary, and we would together welcome in the Christmas season.

But everything in its own time. At the moment, I need solitude, snow, and ice.

The shoveled expanse is long and wide, nearly the size of a hockey rink, though hockey ice is tame and commonplace compared to the ice of a lake. There is wild beauty beneath my skates. Looking down, I see through the utterly clear ice to dark, unlit depths. Small bits of coontail, green and feathery, float in the upper layer of ice. Near shore, the mucky substrate shows regular ridges, the mark of waves roiling beneath a northwest wind, waves stilled now, for a time.

Getting my bearings after nearly ten months off my skates, I flit about, searching for other evidence of life under the ice. We occasionally see leopard frogs doing froggy kicks, like little aquatic bullets, in the shallows. Sometimes bullheads slip by, dark shadows in the darker water. Once, on a skate around the perimeter, we came upon a hapless white-footed mouse trapped under the ice. We guessed it had drowned when venturing unwisely out onto the thinnest possible ice.

I drop to my hands and knees to examine close up the cracks that mar the perfect crystalline lid. The ice is more than four inches thick, a gain of two inches in two days. The increase is the mark of subzero temperatures at night. As a general rule of thumb, we estimate that ice without a snow cover grows by one inch each night below zero. With my face close to the surface, I think I glimpse the pale flash of a fish. Then, another! But I can't seem to get a good look. Slowly,

I repeat the motion and realize that the flash of paleness is the reflection of my own face. The lake is an immense mirror, throwing back images of the frozen world above.

The black ice away from shore beckons. It is both enticing and intimidating—enticing because gliding over its surface feels like silk on skin, intimidating because it is so utterly obvious that it is water, lake water, which is holding me up. I know my far-heavier husband had just been on this ice two days before when it was much thinner. The cracks show me unequivocally that the thickness is DNR-safe. But my body doesn't believe it. Deep in my viscera, I feel a flutter of fear, of excitement, of daring.

Who believes that mere water will support them? Who extends themselves beyond what their senses tell them is prudent? Who, defying their eyes, acts on faith?

Stroke, stroke stroke! I become bolder after I make my first pass down the length of the rink and am not plunged to the murky depths. Stroke, stroke, stroke! The pressure of my two thin blades causes the ice to groan and crack. In one ebony, glossy patch—oh the sheer wildness of it!—the ice, unable to withstand my weight, suddenly readjusts itself. Clear, brittle cracks punctuate the air as white, spidery fault lines scatter outward. And on I fly, still supported by water, transformed water.

There is something cleansing about the cold. It enters one's airways, ears, even the very pores of the skin. It is renewing and life-enhancing. It chases away headaches, worries, and doubts. Forgotten are my frettings over the dinner's timetable, the musical performance at church, the lack of wrapping paper, the disorganization of the household. It all seems so inconsequential now out on the ice. The lake, and its rare, perfect surface, engulfs my concerns.

Out of the confines of the house, away from its warmth

and coziness, I take deep, invigorating breaths. It is thrilling to momentarily break free from conventional expectations of Christmas Eve and its sometimes-cloying sweetness. It is exhilarating to come into a world that is truly wild and beautiful, to have a hint of what it means to really live dangerously, to live as if, on Christmas Eve, God is really with us.

Later in the evening, we hear strange sounds emanating from Pioneer Lake and from the larger North and South Center Lakes. Booms and bellows and high-pitched keening mingle with the Christmas bells of the church. It seems as if the lakes are immense whales, as if they are singing, as if they are serenading us in the beauty of the night.

# Christmas Hockey

Santa had delivered only two hockey sticks to our house the night before, and there are six of us. This is a dilemma, but trifling, really, in the broader scheme of things. Hockey is a rough sport, and if players have to resort to crude equipment, it will be even rougher. The important thing is that we all have skates and we know how to use them. The rink on the lake beckons. Christmas Day is luminous, with hoarfrost glittering on the trees. A weak solstice sun lights the landscape and snow crystals stairstepping down from heaven glint in midair. Off in the distance, the church looks silvery.

Our family has been feasting and singing and opening presents for one full day, with only a short break for sleep. It is time for intermission. Call it cold-air therapy. We need to chase away the lethargy brought on by too much food and too little exercise, too much excitement and too little sleep.

And so, to the rink.

The frosty air rings with our voices as, bundled in polar fleece and sweatshirts, hats and mittens, we shoulder our weapons and tromp down the path to the lake. Someone has rummaged in the garage and located two discarded brooms, modified for broomball. They are fearsome armaments with sawed-off bristles. Tom has found suitable wood in the yard for two other sticks. Real hockey sticks. And though we have a puck or two stashed in the sports equipment bin, we pass on them. We have twelve thousand dollars invested in perfect teeth and no face masks. Instead, we have fished out Missy's dog ball, a small, hard, pink sphere. We need a puck big enough for the real sticks to hit. This, we think, will be Missy's contribution to the game, not anticipating that she has other contributions to make.

John marks out the goals at either end of the rink with large, neon orange cones. We divide ourselves into teams: one parent per team (aging bodies a liability); one daughter per team (each with a feminine reluctance to engage in physical combat); and one son per team (each with no such reluctance). Tom takes one goal and John the other.

Face-off! Andy and Katie, the opposing forwards, scramble for the ball. In sheer bulk, at a college weight of two hundred pounds, none of it fat, Andy has the advantage, but Katie is nimble on skates. Her blonde hair framed by a snowflake-patterned headband, she zips into Andy's path and sweeps at the ball. Within seconds, she outmaneuvers him and takes the ball down rink, across the imaginary blue line. She hesitates and lines up the ball with the goal. She shoots! She scores! Tom, caught off guard, watches the ball bobble past and head merrily down the lake. There are no boards to stop it.

Face-off! Now there are stakes in the game! Andy swings at the ball, and John, who has left his goal to get his whacks in, attempts a stick check. John is about Andy's size, and fiercely competitive. The brothers go at it, and Katie buzzes (wisely) outside the fracas. Christina glides up to poke at the ball and send it down ice. Out of bounds!

It soon becomes apparent that strategy is limited on teams with three players, and brooms, sticks, and balls for equipment. It may be possible to stick-handle the ball down ice. It is less easy to pass to your teammate, provided you have a teammate anywhere in sight. One teammate alternates between defense and forward. The third teammate ought to be back tending goal but often is drawn into battle, which is when points are scored in the untended goal. Play must be halted while the ball is retrieved when an exuberant shot has sent it skittering over the ice. We soon forego face-offs—there would be too many. We put the ball into play from the sidelines, as in basketball. Our hockey game morphs into a sports amalgam.

Christina and I let the forwards do most of the work. Neither of us wants to get jostled, especially on skates. Still, I find myself breathless after pursuing the ball up and down the rink. To rest up, I guard the goal and John glides to center ice. In the goal, I am treated to the sight of brawny Andy rushing at me with one of the sticks, resembling perhaps a caveman on skates, furiously intent on whacking the ball through the cones.

On the sidelines, Missy barks herself hoarse. She is captive to her Shetland sheepdog genes. She must round us up. She trots back and forth, back and forth, tracing the action, barking, barking. She is alternately a vociferous cheerleader and an enraged crowd. She spurs us on to victory!

John scores a goal! Andy scores a goal! The other team pulls its goalie and Tom scores a goal! Ding dong merrily on high, in heav'n the bells are ringing! Ding dong verily the sky is riv'n with angel singing! Gloria!

# Morning Star

The mornings following Christmas are some of the darkest of the year. Although the days begin lengthening immediately after the winter solstice, the added daylight comes at the end of the day. The sun continues to rise later and later for almost three weeks. Not even the faintest trace of pink rims the eastern sky as I peer out the kitchen window at six thirty each morning. We eat a subdued breakfast, each of us thinking it would be better to be in bed. I light a single candle at the table, hoping to kindle a bit of life into the meal that breaks our nightly fast.

It is the Christian Church's season of Epiphany, the time of revelation. The season opens with a focus on a star, the fabled Star of Bethlehem that hangs over a small town, revealing the presence of the Christ Child. From the beginning with this singular light source, the season grows in illumination. At the yellow brick church, we mark the progression of the season by lighting candles on our community's table, the altar, adding flames in each successive week until, by Epiphany's end, the chancel sparkles with fire.

It has been a tough winter this year, this Epiphany. In January, people seemed to be dying in great numbers. Fourteen deaths in the congregation in as many days. Frequently, a pile of earth in the cemetery marked a new grave. I bought and sent a continuous stream of sympathy cards; Tom and I paid calls to the visitations held at the local funeral homes.

Every nearby town has only one. We know our way around all of them.

In my family, the nonfatal version of death—disease and decrepitude—sprang up. My aging father, nearly crippled from arthritis, underwent a total hip replacement, rendering him a shut-in for many weeks. My child, also suffering from arthritic symptoms, was diagnosed with a serious chronic illness. Some mornings I rose feeling permanently shrouded in darkness.

The daylight, when it finally crept over the landscape, was often subdued and muted by cloud cover. This was very unlike Januarys of the past, which are historically bitterly cold and sunny. The brittle air rings with clarity. This January, however, climate change demonstrated that it has us by the throat, as week after week passed with soft gray days above freezing. At another time, the winter warmth might have been a cause of bleak despair. Consumed as I was by my worries in the human realm, I only gave the odd weather the briefest recognition and soldiered on.

Sometime late in January, the persistent cloud cover eased. Coming into the kitchen at my customary time, I noticed a solitary morning star rising on the eastern horizon in advance of the sun. In the darkness that was still night, it gleamed with great beauty. I recognized it as Venus.

This closest planet to us in the solar system is the most similar in size to our earth and considered our "twin." It is often the first celestial body to appear in the sky at sunset, an evening star, or the last to fade at dawn, a morning star. It takes its name from the Roman goddess of beauty, and appropriately so, for nothing is lovelier in the twilight at the end or the beginning of a day than this brilliant, reflected light.

Dreary and difficult as these Epiphany mornings were, it became a habit of mine to look for the star as I entered the kitchen each morning. Switching on the light, I'd move to the window, check the temperature reading on the outdoor thermometer, and locate Venus, my companion in the early hour. I had never so scrupulously observed a star before, and I was astonished by its quick pace across the heavens. Each morning it was noticeably higher than it had been at the same time the day before. Soon it seemed to be hanging from the limbs of our tall cottonwood tree in the southeastern corner of our yard.

I cannot express how much pleasure it gave me to be greeted each morning by this small spectacle of beauty. I looked at Venus as a talisman of sorts, an epiphanous light, and a constant reminder that somewhere Out There, beyond the somber reality of my rather grim winter, was inconceivable glory.

For millennia, people have been guided by the heavens. The starry night sky, unfurled in all its splendor, can take one's breath away. The stars have been a compass, a celestial map to travelers, and often, though perhaps superstitiously, considered portents of significant events. Here on Pioneer Lake, the nights are still dark enough to reveal the Milky Way, that galaxy of far-flung stars that undulates directly overhead each night. Our family takes great pleasure in this. When out of doors in the dark, we often pause to pick out the familiar constellations: the Big and Little Dippers, Cassiopeia, Orion in the winter, and the Summer Triangle.

That the swift movement of Venus across the sky this winter surprised me, however, indicates how little heed I've paid to this major feature of nature. I can recognize some of the circumpolar constellations, those that appear to revolve around the North Star. I can pick out the North Star, Polaris, no matter where I am in the Northern Hemisphere. Thanks to an eighth grade astronomy unit taught by enthusiastic

Mrs. Rohwedder, I am conversant with the zodiacal constellations in the planetary belt, but don't ask me to point
out Spica or Regulus.

My ignorance ought to be a source of shame. If I had been
an Ojibwe woman living on Pioneer Lake two hundred years
ago, I'm sure I'd know the minute details of the celestial display and the seasonal changes occurring there. But comfortable as I am in my warm house lit by electricity, I seldom
spend long periods of time outdoors at night, stargazing. In
winter, I deem it too cold; in summer, too mosquito-infested.
Somehow, the spring and the fall fly by without my attempt
to get to know the stars better. I lump maps of the night sky
in the same category as hand-knitted sweaters: artifacts of
skills I'd like to possess but am too lazy to pursue rigorously.

If I had any sense of urgency in learning the constellations, I'd do it now, for our dark night is fading. With each
new housing development springing up in the cornfields
near us come streetlights, yard lights, lit houses, and increasing numbers of headlights. There seems to be an incessant
human need to banish the darkness. Nearby Lindstrom, a
burg of only three thousand people, lights up its Main Street,
U.S. Highway 8, to the luminosity of day. Some might feel
that comforting, but it unnerves me to drive through town
at midnight on a return trip from the Cities. The stores are
closed, the streets are deserted, and brightness glows like
noon on a dark day.

Astronomers have been vocal in their dismay over the
loss of the night sky. The fainter stars have disappeared altogether in some areas. Artificial lighting threatens even remote
sites where the biggest research telescopes are located. On
cloudy nights, the effect of night lighting is intensified, particularly with a snow cover. Light bounces off the white
snow, off the low-hanging clouds, and creates a phenomenon

known as "sky glow." On a winter night in our yard, we can detect the presence of Lindstrom, Shafer, Taylors Falls, North Branch, and the Wild Mountain ski slopes. How long will it be before our sky is as eerily pink as the suburbs to our south?

The omnipresent invasiveness of light pollution has spawned the new scientific field of "artificial light ecology" and a whole wealth of new terms, such as "light trespass"— when someone's illumination crosses property line—and three types of "glare." It has also inspired pioneering studies on how intense sky glow and direct night lighting affect wildlife. Sea turtles in Florida, for example, are confused by bright hotel lights as they scramble up on beaches to lay eggs. In the absence of darkness, nocturnal frogs do not croak and hence fail to attract mates. Even small animals submerged in water are affected. The tiny aquatic crustaceans in Pioneer migrate upward to the surface to feed on algae each evening. But if they can detect light—say, from a boathouse or a yard light at the beach—they won't make the trip, which may affect their predation on algae, leading in turn to a possible explosion of the algal population.

This is troubling, to be sure. But can anyone measure how the loss of the stars will change our sense of ourselves?

The immensity of the night sky has been an overwhelming experience for people since antiquity. "When I look at your heavens, the work of your fingers, the moon and the stars that you have established, what are humans that you are mindful of them?" the Psalmist asks. Certainly, searching the night sky makes one realize that earthly woes are puny and temporal in the large expanse of the universe.

The constellations we have overhead in our Minnesota night sky can be seen throughout the Northern Hemisphere and give stargazers a tangible fix on what latitude they stand upon that is much different from merely looking at a map.

They are great unifiers, linking Old and New Worlds. Once when on a plane winging its way across the northern Atlantic on an October night, I looked out to see Orion splayed across the heavens, making the long journey with me. I think of Orion as a mark of home, home in the fall and winter. Seeing Orion out the plane window, arcing overhead, made me realize that the whole planet was my home, the starry skies a shared canopy.

The pulsating lights of the stars and the planets—so far away, and veiling so much that we don't know!—have been a reliable reality check since the beginning of time, putting us in our place, making us realize how insignificant we humans are in the great scheme of the world. When our electric lights have obscured all this, what will we have to tell us our place, to let us know that humans are much less important than we think we are?

The stars are our epiphany lights, revealing us to ourselves and linking us to others. So this winter, I watch my morning star adorn the east each new day. Another child recently left to study in France, half a continent and an ocean away. She is in the Old World, speaking in a different tongue, writing words that I, who write volumes, never scribble. In a letter, I mention Venus is a morning star and tell her to look for it as she eats her breakfast. She will see its beauty before I do, but in the Mediterranean sky it will be visible. "We see the same stars," I write to her. We live on the same planet. We are not so far apart. Great beauty illuminates us both.

> How lovely shines the morning star!
> In twilight sky it gleams afar.
> The reign of night is ended.
> Creation stirs to hail its light
> Whose glories now with radiance bright

Stream forth in beauty splendid.
Both far, and near
All things living thanks are giving,
Praise outpouring.
Earth and sky the Lord adoring.

—Burkhard Wiesenmeyer's text to the Epiphany hymn
   "Wie Schön Leuchtet" (1640)

# Geese on the Ice

We first saw the geese shortly before Christmas. In the gray light of a Sunday afternoon, our family went down to the lake to skate half an hour before supper. The north end of Pioneer had been frozen for several weeks, but a persistent patch of water had remained open until a few days before. Subzero temperatures had finally capped it, and we felt confident to head out over its glossy surface.

As the girls and I dallied over our skate laces, using the disassembled dock as a warming bench, the boys raced away, the anxious Sheltie at their heels. They soon reappeared with a report: the ice was smooth down to Grandstrand's, the cracks looked to run four inches thick, and there were six geese sitting on the surface at the point. Tom explained, "They look like oddballs. One's all white, and one might have a broken wing."

Only three days ago there had been a flock of more than a hundred geese on the open water of Pioneer. Interspersed between the buff and black Canada geese had been one pure white bird, a stray domestic that had joined up with its wild cousins. "This is not good," Audubon friends of ours had remarked over coffee. "Some years back, there was a farm goose on Pioneer, and when the lake froze, the bird was caught in the ice and died. They can't fly, you know."

Since then, I'd been keeping an eye on the white goose

and its compatriots. When the open water closed, the flock had disbanded, and I had assumed the birds had taken off for the bigger lakes that were still open. Apparently, all had but six: the white goose, the one with the broken wing, Broken Wing's mate (probably), and three others.

If I had the judicious heart of a true scientist, the situation wouldn't have distressed me. Minnesota's Canada goose population has swelled in the past several decades to nuisance numbers. A large percentage no longer migrates to the species' historic wintering grounds but remains on waters kept artificially open by power plants or aerators. Their vast numbers deposit even vaster droppings on lakeshores and picnic areas and pollute the water with *E. coli*. Five Canada geese stranded on an iced-over lake should be called "natural selection," not "tragic."

Life would be much easier for me if I did not respond sympathetically to the plight of small creatures. But the report of stranded geese (and one with a broken wing) made my stomach knot. What would they eat? How could they keep safe from predators? Still, what could I do to help the dumb clucks? My skates laced, I stood up and headed north, toward the alder thicket and away from the doomed birds, putting distance between me and their fate.

Christmas came and with it the festivities of the season. The college kids arrived from school, bringing great baskets of dirty clothes and youthful zest. We had parties, we had feasts, we had glogg and aquavit, and I put the geese out of my mind.

On New Year's Eve, my brother-in-law stopped by. "Say, I see you've got geese on Pioneer," he remarked. He said it in hushed tones, as one might say, "I hear so-and-so's cancer is terminal." My stomach did a little flip as if to say, "Oh, yeah, *those* birds . . . they're still alive!" Then the conversation turned to his remarkably fruitless ice fishing, and I forgot them once more.

Christmas passed and Epiphany arrived, the season of light. A true Arctic chill settled over east central Minnesota, and we awoke each morning to temperatures far below zero, minus twenty degrees, minus twenty-five. Goldfinches and pine siskins clustered around the bird feeder, voraciously consuming seeds. January compensates for its frigid temperatures by providing us with clear sunny days of increasing length. I had bought a pair of slender skate skis shortly after Christmas, and I began spending time on the flat terrain of frozen Pioneer to teach myself the new sport.

You see different things skiing on a snowy lake than you do skating on ice. Skate skiing around Pioneer at a laborious beginner's pace, I noticed tracks. I looked behind me at the somewhat uneven, but nonetheless distinctive, herringbone marks that a skate skier lays down. I saw the tidy trail the Sheltie left as she dogged my progress around the shoreline. Along the east and north shores, I traveled alongside tracks left by an otter. I could see little round depressions made by its short, stubby legs, and long, concave half-tunnels created as the animal slid along on its belly. Step-step, slide; step-step, slide, an otter tango on Pioneer Lake.

As I passed beneath the hulking form of the church on the south end and took the corner, heading north once more, I caught sight of big bird tracks, each toe at least two inches in length. I wondered fleetingly about eagles, but I hadn't seen a bald eagle since the Christmas Bird Count. Another track showed more clearly the webbing between the toes. They were goose tracks, geese waddling about on the ice!

"They're still alive," I thought again.

The tracks led up a small bank to a yard and there, huddled down and fluffed out, were the geese. They were all facing south, their creamy-feathered breasts soaking up whatever warmth a January sun could bestow. Out of the wind and in the sunshine, they were in as comfortable a spot as could be found on Pioneer that morning.

As soon as I approached, they rose as one and drifted away, as geese do, apparently nonchalant, not exposing the underlying wariness that provoked them to leave such a cozy spot. Honking softly and wiggling their tail feathers, they wafted into a line of fir trees. They were markedly thinner than geese I had seen in November. One or two extended their wings, as if considering flight. I wondered if they were too weak.

How many calories does a goose burn at minus twenty-five degrees? I couldn't imagine. Body temperature for birds is higher than our ninety-eight degrees Fahrenheit, ten degrees higher in many cases. That's about a one-hundred-thirty-degree temperature difference between the internal core of the bird and the outside air. Goose down and feathers are highly efficient insulation, but still, I thought their caloric needs must be immense.

At this point in the narrative, true biologists would say, "Life's tough, it really is," before skiing home to a lunch of soup and grilled cheese sandwiches. I envy them their indifference.

I stood on the ice, distressed by the plight of the geese and cast about in my mind for something that could be done. Should I call the conservation officer? What would I say? "There're six geese out on Pioneer"? He might come out and shoot them. I thought that might be okay; it would end their suffering. But conservation officers have horrific workloads. Six miscalculating geese were hardly worth his attention. There might come a day when I'd really want the conservation officer to pay heed to me. I didn't want to use up my currency.

I would feed the geese. That was something I could do. Wild creatures are adapted to withstand Minnesota winters if they have access to food. Canada geese fatten up in the fall in harvested cornfields, gleaning kernels fallen amid the stubble. We had cracked corn at home. I could spread it on the ice. I skied home, found a bucket, and scooped corn into it, then trotted on the ice back to the spot where I'd seen the most tracks. I scattered the corn on the ice and returned home. I tried to forget about them.

Over lunch, I wondered about the ragged edges of the story: how is it that able-bodied geese misread winter's cues and remained on the frozen lake? How could loyalty to a mate override the self-preserving instincts to migrate? How much wildness remains in a domesticated goose that leaves a barnyard stocked with food to join its wild kin? And the question that frayed me the most: what role, if any, should a human play in this natural drama?

This question has plagued me since my graduate days in the laboratories at the university. What is the proper relationship between people and wild animals? The Christian Church has one answer, derived from the Genesis account of creation: humans are the crown of creation, lords over the other, lesser, creatures. Adam demonstrates this when he gives the other animals names. In Genesis, God intones: "Have dominion over the fish of the sea and over the birds of the air and over every living thing."

Evolutionary biology offers a different perspective: humans are one of many animals, part of the great web of life. They are not a "crown" of anything, but one highly adapted animal among a biological network of millions, all evolved to a specific niche. This view is what biologists hold in theory, but when it comes to research, they act under the assumptions of Genesis. Animals are trapped, netted, collared, killed. In the lab they are dissected, macerated, probed, and pickled.

As a young graduate student, I tagged along on a research project that studied the migration patterns of a population of meadow mice. Movement into and out of the study plot was recorded for individual mice. The little furry creatures, all brown and all the same size, were identified by a specific pattern of clipped toes. Meadow mice have five toes on each forepaw and four toes on each hindpaw. With one toe clipped on a forepaw and one clipped on a hindpaw, the various combinations can identify a large number of mice. It was common practice in work with small mammals twenty years ago. I'm sure it was painful for the mice to lose a toe, but apparently they survived the trauma. Mice marked in this manner were recaptured many times over the seven-year course of the study.

Mary, the older graduate student conducting the study for her doctorate, was not indifferent to the procedure. "For one thing," she told me one morning out in the field, "we don't know how missing a toe affects the little guys. Does the wound ever get infected and kill some? Do they have a shortened life span without a toe or two?"

I winced with each snip of the scissors and didn't do doctoral work involving mammals. Instead, I chose a project that used an invertebrate as a study animal, thinking it would be easier to kill or maim something that resembled an insect. Strangely, this didn't prove true. Recall—to a biologist, all animals are part of the great web of life. On the evening that I received my degree, at my celebratory party, I raised a glass to toast the thousands of small sow bugs that had been sacrificed for my research. My family and friends thought I was joking, but I was not.

Biologists like to say that the engine that drives scientific research is pure, unadulterated curiosity. Scientists, the common wisdom goes, have a consuming thirst to find answers to the questions they ask. I was never sure that satisfying my curiosity sufficiently justified all the havoc wreaked on animal lives in the name of science. I left the university, doctorate in hand, thinking I had been a failure as a scientist.

Twenty years later, I still have no answer to this. In order to accrue biological knowledge, scientists have to kill animals and plants. Sometimes studies can be conducted no other way. Even in live studies, our clumsiness and life's fragility cause many accidental deaths. What we have learned from our scientific endeavors has improved the quality of human life, explained genetics, helped us better protect biological communities and identify and preserve endangered species. My appreciation of science's great gifts does not jibe with my reluctance to impose suffering or death on its test animals.

Each day now, I ski around the lake. It hasn't snowed in awhile, so tracks are accumulating. I follow my herringbone marks, I note the busy otter. When I reach the geese domain, I note how they've tamped down the snow with their webbed feet, how some of my cracked corn has been eaten. The birds leave droppings on the ice, and I suspect a neighbor is also feeding them. The lake will be frozen another two and one-half months. Will they survive the winter?

I also see my own footprints leading from our shoreline to the geese. Back and forth, back and forth they go. It may be foolish, but I reason that there is so much suffering, so much need in this world, I cannot possibly address all of it. This one small thing I can do. Though I'd like to profess that humans are merely one part of the great web of life, the Genesis truth of our great power over the rest of creation needs to be acknowledged. It is a mark of maturity to step up to its responsibility.

Uneasy is the head that wears the crown.

# Passing the Salt

When the phone rang on a snowy afternoon two years ago, the voice on the other end said, "Mrs. Leaf? This is Officer Anderson from the Chisago County Sheriff's Department calling. There's been an accident on Highway 8, but I want you to know that your son is okay."

Highway 8 is known as a treacherous road. It averages about one fatal accident a year. A phone call from the county sheriff is what every local parent most fears. I could barely hear above the throbbing of my heart as the officer proceeded to tell me that John had spun out on the busy highway on his way home from school. Fortunately, no one had been coming from the other direction. Ours was the only car involved. John was "pretty shook up," and I could come and get him at the Middle School where he and the officer were waiting in the parking lot.

I pulled on boots and jacket, grabbed my car keys, and was out the door in a minute. It had been snowing most of the day, not heavily, but steadily. I had not been out yet and was surprised to find the roads snowpacked and fairly slick. My antilock brakes kicked in as I approached the stop sign at the turn-off to Highway 8. As I eased my car on to the trunk highway, I could see that even this major road was thick with compressed snow.

A mile away, the family minivan could be seen hunkered

down in the school lot. The front bumper had been pulled out, and the car seemed to snarl at me as I drove alongside it. John was ashen and hunched over the wheel, looking young and vulnerable, lacking hat and gloves, his letter jacket clearly inadequate to handle winter weather. He had gotten his driver's license the previous spring. Thoughtful and cautious by nature, he had always been a careful driver, and the officer was quick to say that he probably hadn't been speeding. Most likely, he'd just been traveling too fast for the road condition. When he'd begun to fishtail, he panicked and hit the brakes, which sent him into a spin. The rotating car took out four guard posts, but these saved him from rolling over into South Center Lake. The minivan could be driven, but on closer inspection I discovered that every single panel and both bumpers had sustained damage.

Nearly all Minnesotans driving in the winter can relate a similar drama. Youth and inexperience, or quickly changing road conditions when the air temperature is at the freezing point—one way or another, drivers slip, slide, skid, and spin on snowy roads. The officer had this parting comment: in the ten years he'd been patrolling Highway 8, he'd never seen the road in such poor shape. Usually the state plows made passes every twenty minutes with a snowfall like this one. This afternoon, he hadn't seen one.

There had been talk that with the state budget extremely tight, the Minnesota Department of Transportation (MnDOT) had initiated new plowing guidelines, and the snowpacked condition of dangerous Highway 8 was the result. We inquired about this and were told that no, there had not been changes made to the maintenance of the highway. The accident highlighted for us how utterly dependent we are on the prompt removal of snow from our roads, not only for our safety but for our deepest happiness. Off the top of my head, I can name four recent fatalities on Highway 8. That afternoon, it could have been John.

Thump, thump, thump, thump. My Adidas beat a steady tattoo on the pavement as I head out on my daily run. I'm a fitness runner with no claim to great prowess, but each week I spend about three hours traversing the county roads running through the countryside surrounding Pioneer Lake. I see things that most nonrunning Minnesotans do not.

If I head south as I start my run, the first building I pass, on my left, is the county highway garage. The highway garage is a good neighbor to us. It keeps its lights off at night so there's not excessive light pollution. We are always assured of being the first road plowed after a storm, and I like to think that road crews are more attentive to the cavernous potholes that appear just outside their driveway entrance. But frequently as I pass the two entry points to the garage in the winter, I encounter small drifts of bluish salt crystals lining the verge of the road, or tracing the route of the salter/sander dump truck as it headed out to tend to the roads. In the course of the winter, the sand that's mixed with the salt accumulates in the ditches and along the road. The salt dissolves and runs off—salt crystals don't pile up like sand grains.

As I run, I have time to ponder what happens to the salt. Salt is water-soluble—this is pointing out the obvious—and salt laid down in the watershed of Pioneer Lake ends up in the lake. On melting days, I can see this happening, as small rivulets of melt water trickle through the culverts in the ditches, all headed toward the basin. On other days, the salt forms a thin white crust over the asphalt or the stones of the verge. For the time being, it has crystallized out. But it's not going to go away; salt is a stable compound.

Last fall on my daily outings around the neighborhood, I kept my eye on a newly laid strip of sod that covered the southern edge of Hillside Cemetery, flanking Chisago County Road 37. The minor thoroughfare received a major overhaul two summers ago—widened, resurfaced, even curbed and guttered along the cemetery land. When the work was finished, four or five strips of lush green sod were placed to repair the damage done to the cemetery lawn.

The new grass was watered by great tankers throughout the fall, and yet the following April, as the countryside freshened into verdure, the sod emerged from the snow piles a pale, hay-like color. It was deader than dead. All through the winter, plows had thrown up a briny mix, casting it over the new sod. The young plants, struggling to gain a toehold, couldn't make it. I found the death of the sod disconcerting, but more worrisome was what wasn't visible. The south shore of Pioneer Lake is less than fifty feet to the west of the cemetery. Its shoreline had received several dump truck loads of large, limestone-like boulders for the landscaping following road construction. No doubt this was done to protect the shoreline from erosion. But vegetation is much better at sopping up runoff and preventing its salt load from reaching the lake. The rocks have no effect, none, on the salt entering the basin.

A school child could tell you that salt is made up of equal parts sodium and chlorine. A high school chemistry student would add that it comes apart completely in water into ions that can be taken up by plants.

It is not uncommon to come across a strip of dead or dying vegetation along a busy road. Evergreen trees and shrubs are especially susceptible to the salty spray that vehicles kick up as they pass by. Last winter, a large white pine that had graced the yard of Lindstrom's historic Dinnerbell

Restaurant for probably a hundred years sickened and died. The tree was within the spray of brine coming off Highway 8, and before it actually succumbed, passersby on the highway watched it gradually go under, one graceful bough at a time.

Salt creates an artificial drought for the trees. Evergreens actually take it in through their needles. Chloride ions move into their cells, and the trees require more water to dilute the high concentrations. Unlike deciduous trees that go dormant in the winter, evergreens carry on low-level life processes. Excess chloride impedes these, to the point of death.

Salt also damages roadside soils. Sodium, dissolved in water, destroys the soil structure and reduces its ability to retain water. If soils can't adequately act as a sponge to melt water, they become much more susceptible to erosion.

Pioneer Lake's aquatic ecosystem, too, is under assault from road salt. About an eighth of its shoreline is now reinforced by sterile, nonproductive rock, with no natural vegetation. The small, microscopic animals that are an essential part of the lake's food chain confront regular salt inputs. Researchers know that certain organisms have toxic cutoff points, measured in milligrams of salt per liter of water. A toxic dose is the result of both how much pollutant is in the water and how long it stays there. A Minnesota research Web site states that probably the "effects [of salt] are small" on lakes and ponds, compared to other pollutants running into them. Apparently, no one has undertaken an area-wide study that specifically targets the impact of road salt on lakes and streams.

Neighboring Wisconsin, however, does have one pertinent study. Lake Mendota, situated in Madison, Wisconsin, and adjacent to the university, has been minutely scrutinized by generations of university students. Mendota has been accumulating salt at a rate of 0.3 milligrams per liter of water per year, since 1910. That date marks the advent of the automobile. And since 1962, the rate of salt deposition has doubled, to 0.6 milligrams per liter per year. Sixth-tenths of a milligram added to each liter of water is not very much, but it is a measurable amount, and what worries me is that there is no endpoint in sight. With a certain salt concentration, lakes become unable to "turn over"—that is, they no longer experience the twice-yearly mixing of water and nutrients that occurs when the top layer of water sinks and the lower levels rise to the surface. Turnover is essential for the healthy functioning of a temperate-zone lake. Lakes that can't turn over are dead.

What runs off into Pioneer is not yet at harmful levels, but if we continue to use salt indefinitely—and at what point might we stop?—we will in a hundred years, in two hundred years, at some point, damage its ecosystem beyond repair.

There *is* a waterway in Minnesota that is at the point of ecological impairment from road salt: Shingle Creek. Shingle Creek is a sizable stream draining a flat, sandy watershed in the northern suburbs of Minneapolis and emptying into the Mississippi River. Measurement of its chlorine content shows it to have chronic, toxic levels of the ion, thought to be due to decades of receiving deicing salt from suburban roads. The creek now has a water pollution reduction plan aimed at decreasing the salt input from roads.

Minnesota's Department of Transportation is not indifferent to the threat of salt to our precious lakes. MnDOT has developed the deicing of roads into a fine science and in the process has received worldwide recognition for its expertise. The department regularly engages in professional exchanges with other countries that also wrestle with balancing road safety and environmental protection. MnDOT has detailed graphs that display the guidelines by which salt and sand are laid down, depending on the temperature of the pavement and the weather conditions. They began a salt-reduction pilot project a decade ago that has since been adopted state-wide. In part, the project was initiated as bellwethers such as Shingle Creek began to ring out alarms. And in part, this was pursued to save money: Minnesota spends between six and eight million dollars each year on road salt—and the cost will continue to rise as salt mines are depleted.

Eight million dollars seems an improbable cost for salt. After all, salt is cheap. A twenty-six-ounce box of Morton's table salt ("When it rains, it pours") can be had at our local grocer's for sixty-eight cents. But the amount of salt applied to deice a road is unfathomably large: two hundred pounds per two-lane mile—two hundred pounds per mile!—at thirty degrees; eight hundred pounds per two-lane mile in colder temperatures. Highway 8 is twenty-two miles long, so that is forty-four hundred pounds of salt, more than two tons. For just one mild-temperature snowfall. Imagine all the salt that enters the environment each winter—coming off all the federal freeways, the state highways, the county and town-ship roads, and the city streets.

In the course of its research to lessen its reliance on salt, MnDOT has discovered that applying liquid chemicals *before* a snowfall (or an "event," as the department calls it) prevents snow and ice from bonding to the pavement. This process, called "brining," greatly reduces overall salt use. Brining is practiced on all state highways. It is not uncommon to come upon the lumbering orange MnDOT vehicles spraying out liquid as skies appear leaden, before a single flake falls.

Now I need to admit here that I have long been a covert worshiper of the snowplow. A bulky orange form, a blinking blue light ahead on the highway on a snowy night induce in me a profound reverence and gratitude. At the same time, I seize with terror at the prospect of one approaching me on an icy road, well aware of its ability to instantaneously wipe out my existence. When I encounter a plow laying down brine, I assume the attitude appropriate to any deity: "Thank you, O Great Snowplow, for your benevolent protection." That these orange gods now seem to at least be aware of their effect on the environment only enhances their deific nature.

Could the gods use other means to smite the ice? The agrichemical world has been bounteous in its development of alternatives to sodium chloride. Some of these are merely other compounds in the salt category: magnesium chloride, calcium chloride. But others are new brews, some based on corn extracts and others on sugar cane. These have the benefit of being biodegradable and nontoxic to plants. They also do not corrode pavement, bridges, and other highway structures.

Sadly, the additive put into these alternatives that makes them noncorrosive contains large quantities of phosphorus. The phosphorus content, hundreds to ten thousands of times greater than that of plain salt, which has virtually no phosphorus, means that alternatives pollute lakes in a different kind of way. Most of them are costly, too—three times more than salt.

A few weeks ago, I walked uptown on an extremely cold afternoon. The wind howled from the northwest, blustering across the full expanse of North Center Lake, stinging my skin and watering my eyes. The thermometer on our porch had read ten degrees as I headed out.

On Summit Avenue, high above the lake, gray rutted

piles of snow lined the thoroughfare. In one was a small pool of water. I actually passed the puddle before I stopped, thought, "Water?" and backtracked. I hesitated a minute, then pulled off a mitten and stuck my index finger into the pool and tasted: salty. Quite salty. It must have been loaded with salt, in fact, to depress the freezing point of water twenty degrees. The outside air was not much warmer than that of a deep freeze. Imagine maintaining a cup of liquid water inside your freezer.

Eventually, the water in the puddle will evaporate, leaving behind the salt. The salt will not break down by sunlight or bacteria, or any other natural agent that we unconsciously rely on to clean up our messes. It will instead form a lacy, white crust that, with the first thunderstorm of spring, will be redissolved and washed away, carried with the coursing rainwater down the hill and into the lake. This will happen again and again, with every snowfall, with every rainfall, this year and the next year and the next, for as long as we require snow- and ice-free roads for our safety.

Where do we draw the line between our own safety and convenience, and the overall, long-term health of our lakes, those bodies of fresh water of which we are so proud? I don't have an answer to this question. Our society routinely steals from the future. In this instance, the theft is fresh water. Somehow, that seems particularly egregious.

# Winter Geography

I am always a little sad the day after the deadline for removing fish houses from the lakes. In the Chisago Lakes area, we get accustomed to the geography of the temporary villages that bloom on the ice in December. We keep an eye on the activity of ice village life throughout the long weeks of winter. The demise of the ice villages signals the end of winter's worst. It is a punctuation mark in the year, sharing kinship with the last day of school and Labor Day, two other endings with which the door clangs shut on a familiar daily routine and opens on to a new season.

Pioneer Lake never has fish houses—who would go to all that work for bullheads?—but North and South Center Lakes are well populated each winter. The villages appear at roughly the same spots from year to year, but not always. This year, North Center had a sizeable colony far down the northwest end of the lake, something I don't recall seeing before.

The first village to emerge on any of the six Chisago Lakes springs up on the easternmost bay of South Center, where it connects to the larger part of the lake. That section of South Center must be shallow and sheltered from wind and wave action, because it freezes early, earlier than the other big lakes. People even appear on that bay before the rest of the lake has frozen over. I am frequently shocked to see a camper pickup—maybe the same camper pickup, driven by the same daredevil each year, I don't know—on the ice at an impossibly early date when it seems it shouldn't be safe.

Once the South Center bay has been colonized, a predictable pattern of settlement ensues. First there are people with campstools, crouched over holes, unsheltered from the wind. Then come the trucks and cars that convey anglers to their unsheltered holes. And then, one weekend it is deemed safe, and the houses appear, five, ten, twenty all at once, and the lakes assume their winter geography of big villages, little villages, and isolated houses, and often roads running between them, and from each village to an access point on the shoreline.

The appearance of the fish houses is the tangible expression of the full flowering of winter. The party is assembled, let the fun begin!

The movie *Grumpy Old Men* introduced American moviegoers to the concept of ice villages, something I had never thought needed discussing, but I was wrong. The Hollywood depiction of life on the ice apparently left an impression. I once took a raft trip down the roiling Snake River in Wyoming and spent much of the time answering questions from uninitiated Germans who'd seen the film and wondered about people in Minnesota who cut holes in the ice and dropped fishing lines into them. "Ach, ja, Minnesota," they'd said when we'd been introduced. "Where people fish through ice . . . is that true?"

But my favorite story of the improbability of an ice community is of a conversation that occurred at Hazelden, an internationally known drug rehabilitation center that actually overlooks the early-freezing bay of South Center Lake. A friend of mine, known for his wit and humor, was a counselor at Hazelden. He was acting as a mentor to an intern, newly arrived from Saudi Arabia, who found a Minnesota autumn to be a good deal chillier than the desert. One November day, my friend caught the intern staring intently out the window at the lake.

"Is that, is that *ice* forming along the edges?" the Arab asked in disbelieving tones.

"Oh, yeah," replied my friend, who was himself a transplant to the state. "Just wait 'til the locals start driving their cars out on it and set up their houses!"

A shocked silence followed. Then, laughter.

"I get it!" the intern said gleefully. "They told me to watch out for you! They said you were a kidder!"

This year, South Lindstrom had an unusually large village in a new location, just off the point from the swimming beach. By the third Sunday in Advent, there were twenty to thirty fish houses plopped down, and because it was close to Highway 8, I could watch village life each time I drove by.

The weekends, of course, are the liveliest times for ice villages. Even early on Saturday morning, cars and trucks are pulled up to their respective shacks. Occasionally, I'd catch sight of an angler in bright orange or khaki coveralls, or a bulky snowmobile suit, warm hat (earflaps, if present, functional), and thick choppers. A dog might accompany him, frosty breath emanating from both. I might see the characteristic hand movement involved in manipulating a fishing line with deerskin mitts.

On Saturday nights, driving home from the Cities after an evening out at a concert or play, Tom and I would see a sprinkle of pinpoints of light mirroring the sparkle of stars overhead. The villages were occupied, lit by lanterns, by candles, even by electric lights powered by a car battery. Vehicles slowly crawled from shack to shack over the ice, easing their way to solid land. Sometimes, far off in the blackness would be a solitary light, evidence of someone tending a hole in the open, nearly swallowed by the night.

I am not an angler, but my sons are, and they pursue their passion in all seasons. The eldest bought a hand auger for drilling holes through the ice while still in his teens, and over the years Santa has been generous with tip-ups (contraptions by which poles can be left untended), lures, and those peculiar mittens that convert to half-finger gloves. The boys will occasionally spend a Saturday night in someone's fish house on one of the lakes. They rig the tip-ups and set about the equally important business of playing cards or drinking pop. They never bring fish home from these parties, though. Rather, the house, with the warmth of a small heater and the brightness of a kerosene flame, is a great place for a poker party, where boys can be as noisy as they'd like, away from the ears of parents.

Minnesota's Department of Natural Resources decrees that fish houses have to be off the lakes in the southern two-thirds of the state by February 28. The weekend before the deadline, there is a flurry of activity on the lakes, as owners get ready to pull up stakes, as it were, and vacate. As that day approaches, I always think it is a shame that the deadline is so early. On that last weekend, winter still seems in full reign. The ice is solid, the snow pervasive, and the air, cold and crisp.

But it never fails that only a week or so later, there will be a change of wind. Suddenly, the sun seems warmer, the flat lake surface develops pools of water from melting snow, and the wisdom of the DNR is plainer. I have thoughts of honeycombed ice. Honeycombed ice is just what the term implies: ice that has developed pockets of air, ice that has begun to disintegrate under the warmth of a strengthening sun. It looks sound, but it gives way without warning.

Yesterday was March 1. The lakes are bare and wind-swept. No longer occupied and domesticated by ephemeral villages, they have reverted to their wild state. Far out in the middle of South Center, I see a lone, parka-clad figure, walking carefully to shore.

# Lengthening

When does winter turn into spring?

That is the question of the moment. I returned recently from a vacation in southern France. Flying home, from the plane I could see my native land cloaked entirely in snow. All the lakes frozen, big white pennies scattered across Minnesota's face, all the farm fields bright and featureless. The landscape looked more wintry than when we had left, ten days previous. At home, I was disheartened, looking out over the snowy lumps and knobs that were my garden boxes. I had returned with thoughts of pansies and primroses and early leaf lettuce.

Then, mysteriously, the birds returned, although a snowy shroud remained. Five days after we got back, horned larks and robins appeared. The next day, I saw kestrels on the wire and red-winged blackbirds perched on dry cattails in the marsh. Canada geese, tundra swans, red-tailed hawks, eastern bluebirds. I thought the early arrivals had made a dreadful mistake.

Yesterday, I stepped outside just before dawn. It was twenty-two degrees, and the eastern horizon was foggy with moisture from melting snow. Frost rimed every matted blade of grass, the mounds of dirt from whence I had hastily dug carrots last November, and the trellis with the dried remains of last summer's morning glories. It seemed in aspect and temperature like every other morning for the past three months. The crystalline silence of the frost shattered at the flute-like song of a robin. The bird perched at the very top of the cottonwood tree, and as its cheery, melodic voice drifted down, the scales fell from my eyes and I saw it was spring. At that very moment, the winter vanished. The season turned on the robin's singular cadence.

The liturgical season of Lent begins on the cusp between winter and spring. The word itself speaks of nature. *Lent* comes from the Old English root *lengten*, to lengthen. Throughout the season, with the approach of the vernal equinox, it is apparent that the days are getting longer. Lent has very old roots in the Christian Church. It has been observed since the second century as a season of introspection, self-examination, and repentance. Once seen as a period of preparation for entry into the body of believers through baptism on Easter Eve, Lent is now most often a time of spiritual renewal. The disciplines of prayer and meditation and, often, the act of giving up a particular pleasure for the forty-day period mark its passage. It is a time of stripping down to the bare essentials in order to winnow out what is most valuable in life and in relationship.

For believers in the Northern Hemisphere, Lent is inextricably bound to the coming of spring. The two are entangled just as the roots of two closely aligned trees wrap around and about until it is impossible to tell where one ends and the other begins. Lent begins at a time when nature has already stripped down and is garnering what is necessary to continue. The observance of Lent finds its echo in the naked landscape of dormancy.

The season opens near the end of winter. The first day of Lent is marked by ashes, a fit symbol for dead, decayed, and disintegrating life. The hour is dark and the air is sharp as we gather on Wednesday evening to receive the mark of ashes on our foreheads. But in the ensuing six weeks, the days will lengthen and the air will adopt a mild, sweet scent as the earth is released from winter's bondage.

The longer I live, the more I appreciate the Lenten season and the earliest days of spring. With increasing age, I have developed a taste for subtlety rather than gaudy show, and for the dynamic process of becoming rather than the static state of culmination. The early spring of Lent offers both of these at the same time.

My writing desk is at a window that frames a large red maple in our yard. In late March, with patches of snow lingering and Pioneer Lake still solidly frozen, the maple buds, the earliest flowers of a northern spring, have swelled and grown rosy. I can't imagine a more tangible expression of expectancy. As Lent progresses, week by week, I will watch the buds enlarge, the red casings split to reveal the flower, the thread-like stamens standing exposed to the wind, wafting powdery pollen like tiny puffs of smoke. The flowers consist only of stamens and pistils, the necessary parts for a wind-pollinated plant that does not have to attract pollinators by a bright show of colorful petals. The maple flower is a paradigm of modesty and economy. By Easter, the tiny flowers will have burst open, though few will hail their appearance. There could be no more self-effacing bloom.

Later, I will eye the tulips in my rock garden. Tulips, too, are more interesting in process than culmination. I find the tulip bud more aesthetically pleasing than the full-blown flower. Watching it grow from the first peek of a rosy-tipped leaf spearing the cold soil to the mature plant with plump preflowers bowing under the pressure of an April rain is more engrossing than beholding its classic tulip form.

Down at the shore, Pioneer's ice has grown dark and granular. In some areas, where the equinoctial sun bears down, it has given way to water. Narrow bands lap at the shoreline. It is disconcerting to observe the rutted tracks so recently carved out by snowmobiles terminating in a now-open pool. Ice-out is imminent.

Every year, my daughter and her like-minded cousins celebrate the return of open water by donning bikinis and plunging into North Center Lake on the day the ice goes out. They approach the newly released water dressed in sweatpants and shirts, but these they shed as they abandon sense (and sensation) and dive into the thirty-two-degree lake, their blonde heads striking in the weak spring sunlight. I can't help but think that buried deep in their Scandinavian genes resides an imperative that propels them to such an affinity. There is a certain cachet to swimming with ice blocks.

I, too, am ecstatic at ice-out. When the lakes all around us are open, they become immense, living entities. The liquid surfaces dance and dimple. Sunlight bounces off the waves, glinting and winking. Everything near the water looks brighter, lighter, as the lakes serve as giant mirrors. The quality of light changes from that of somber winter to one with sparkle and shine. The open lakes become beasts under the lashing of a spring wind, roaring in gales or chuckling in gentle laps against the lake's edge.

The companionable monster that resides below our hill, the one we call Pioneer, is about to wake from its winter nap. Already I can hear the soft cackle of geese waiting patiently from the shelf of ice. When that happens, winter's pensiveness will turn to joy. The gulls will scream, the geese will chortle, and I will laugh.

# Owl Invasion

In the winter of 2004–2005, Minnesota became the stage for the largest northern owl irruption in recorded history. An irruption is a biological term denoting a rapid, irregular increase in number, and that is what happened in the state. Tens of thousands of owls migrated from Canada southward and continued moving south as the winter progressed. They peaked in number in the vicinity of Pioneer Lake in the midst of Lent, but their story began many months prior.

## The Owls and Santa Lucia

The first report of owls came in November, at the onset of winter. My e-mail messages informed me that there was a spike in number of arctic owls occurring in northern Minnesota. Four species of owls normally seen only in the far north were espied with increasing frequency. The most common ones, those that grabbed people's attention, were the great gray owls—the largest North American owl, with a wing span of nearly six feet—but northern hawk owls, boreal owls, and snowy owls were also invading the state.

The appearance of the owls had a salutary effect on bird-watchers. In the days following the election, the world had grown darker as sunlight bled from the horizon and the bright hours grew short. Bird watching is pleasantly distracting, easing the mind from distressing events, big and small.

The larger presence of owls seemed like a gift from nature. The reports told of owls in great abundance in the northern bogs. People had seen twenty, thirty great gray owls in a day! Ecstatic birders were flocking to the forests to witness the surge.

Owl irruptions are a natural phenomenon. Animal populations show more dramatic swings in the far north—numbers peak, then crash. When mice populations are low, owls migrate south in search of food. Old, experienced birders could name a dozen years or more when they had observed owl irruptions in northern Minnesota, though even in December this increase seemed to be greater than in past years.

A keen but lazy birder, I was intrigued by the prospect of adding four new species to my life list without traveling to Canada. When I received an invitation to a junket headed north to take in the owls, I was thrilled. My excitement lasted for as long as it took me to get home and consult my calendar. I was scheduled to play piano for the annual Santa Lucia Festival put on by the local Swedish heritage club the day of the owl trip. There was slim chance I could find a replacement.

So on the Saturday when my fellow birders were winging their way north, I sat behind a keyboard, one glum German American in a sea of Swedes. The church basement was transformed by sparkling candles, the fragrance of coffee and fruit soup, and the red of Christmas elves and decorative hearts. The sweet children's voices sang "Nu tandes tusen julejus" (A thousand Christmas candles now are lit upon the earth), and I thought, "I have lost the opportunity of a lifetime."

## The Owls and the Prairie

Following the Santa Lucia Festival, when duty had trumped pleasure, we entered a dry period. "A brown winter," meteorologists called it, though my sense of those days was more colorless than brown, and more full of despair than the term would imply. When snow finally came, I was so parched for blessings that I was pathetic in my gratefulness.

The day after the first substantial snowfall, in late January, my husband and I skied at Wild River State Park for the first time. In a very brief span of time, a colorless world became iridescent, each fresh snowflake catching the glint of the sun. Out on the restored prairie, we took in the expansive landscape, our skis singing as we zipped along. We were navigating a turn in the trail that would take us into the woods, when my husband slowed and whispered, "Look—in that tree."

Twenty feet away, at the top of a slender sapling, perched the largest owl I had ever seen: a great gray owl. It seemed too small a tree to support a bird that size, but great gray owls are deceptive. Their bodies have actually less mass than great horned owls, but they are thickly feathered—"the most feathers for the smallest amount of real bird," as one naturalist has remarked. The feathers covering the bird's legs fluffed in the wind. He rotated his head and trained a pair of yellow eyes in our direction. We could see the large, circular feather pattern that ornithologists call the "facial disc," an arrangement that funnels sound toward their ears. What had first seemed all gray became a muted mix of taupe and dun, white and smoke under close scrutiny. It was a beautiful bird.

A blink, and the head swiveled away. The bird simply was not interested in us. I wondered if our presence had even registered on his radar. It was a snub more seamless than an adept hostess might bestow on an obnoxious guest, but we were charmed. With that one smooth motion, it was clear that he had claimed the prairie for Owlhood, and our status had been relegated to that of intruders.

"You see," my husband remarked as we skied away, "sometimes the mountain comes to Mohammed."

### The Owl and the Children

Owls now appeared as if from a scene out of Harry Potter. All were great grays. The other species didn't seem to need to keep on the move. A friend called to say that Pine County to our north harbored an astonishing number of great gray owls. He had seen twenty-eight in one day, nineteen of those shortly before sunset. "We think they're headed south at a rate of twenty-five miles per week," he told me. "They need to eat half their body weight each day, about one pound of mice. They seem to be most active just before sunset, as if they need to catch one more mouse before nightfall."

Wild River Park came alive with owls. Five were seen along the gravel road bordering the park to the west. Two were reported from the Goose Creek area. Two hung out by the guest cabins. One, which soon became the poster child of the irruption, was fond of perching on the speed limit sign at the park entrance.

As the Great Grays moved deeper into human-occupied space, the inevitable happened: many met their demise in confrontations with automobiles. Their tendency to position themselves along open roadsides and their supreme indifference to non-owl matters became their undoing. The slaughter was unprecedented. By mid-January, more than 260 had been killed in Minnesota by cars. Conservation officers thought this figure greatly underrepresented the actual number that had died. The number of birds killed was so great because there were so many great grays present. Biologists estimated that one-tenth of the great gray owl population of North America was spending the winter in Minnesota.

Wildlife specialists did necropsies on some of the dead

great grays and found them to be in seemingly good physical condition. They apparently weren't starving. But they
were stressed. No animal leaves familiar surroundings and
migrates hundreds of miles in winter just for the thrill of
travel.

As the head of our local Audubon chapter, I wrote a
letter to the newspaper, alerting the community to the invading owls, extolling their charms, asking people to drive
slowly at dusk, and urging them to visit the park to see this
natural phenomenon. Several weeks later, at the park with
a friend, we encountered a station wagon parked by the
speed limit sign. A mother and four girls in pink parkas were
in the road, exclaiming over an owl perched on a nearby
shrub. They were so excited, as thrilled as I was, I'm sure,
when I saw the first owl, on the prairie.

By this time, the great grays at Wild River had become
celebrities. They'd been on TV newscasts, in both Twin Cities
papers, and even in the pages of *Newsweek*. Birders from all
over the United States were coming to see the owls. This
owl, probably the poster child, didn't ignore the girls. As the
children waved their arms, the bird lifted off, exhibiting the
six-foot wingspan, and flew to the top of a pine fifty yards
away. "Ooh!" the children exclaimed and ran after it, their
unzipped jackets flapping, their boots crunching the snow.

I looked on anxiously. Stressed animals are very close to
the edge. Any extra expenditure of energy, any disturbance
from noise or human presence might have disastrous effect
on a weakened bird. Somehow, when I envisioned people
trekking to the park to see the owls, I hadn't imagined noise
and waving arms. Should I speak to the mother? Say something to the kids? I didn't want to be a killjoy. I remembered
my own childhood. When an adult reprimanded me, I was
crushed—sometimes permanently.

It was after sunset. The family would be leaving within minutes and the bird would be at peace. The incident troubled me—but why couldn't I speak for the owl?

## The Owls and the Prayer Breakfast

The next morning, I was once again behind a piano keyboard, this time to accompany hymns at a community-wide Lenten prayer breakfast. "Awake my soul, and with the sun, thy daily stage of duty run," the people sang, while I thought about owls. The light in the sanctuary was still muted. Despite the increasing brightness accompanying the spring equinox, sunlight had not yet penetrated the inner space of the church. The worshipers, lacking their morning coffee, were sleepy. During the homily, I scanned the order of service to anticipate what would follow, and I saw under "The Prayers" a directive informing us that we would be invited to offer petitions. Out loud.

This was an instruction our pastors would only issue to an ecumenical bunch like those at the community breakfast. In a Lutherans-only assembly, the silence during a prayer free-for-all would be deafening. We have a shared horror of revealing anything as personal as an inward spiritual life. Spirituality for Lutherans is a private matter, more private even than sex.

The prayers began: "Let us pray for the whole people of God in Christ Jesus and for all people according to their needs: we pray for your world. . . . we pray for our nation. . . . we pray for the sick and dying. . . . we pray for creation. . . ." Creation?! My heart stopped. Who will offer a petition for creation? Who is better informed to offer a prayer for nature than I? What would I say? "We pray for the owls . . . ?" People would think, "The owls?!"

If I didn't offer a petition, someone else would step in

and make a conventional and meaningless request, probably asking that we be "good stewards" of all that we have
been "given." I can't say how much this irritates me. What
is a steward, really? No one has stewards in the twenty-first
century. Not even Northwest Airlines has stewards anymore—they're all flight attendants. Should I ask that we all
be good . . . ? No, I wouldn't even go there.

I offered a silent prayer: that the owls remain safe from
human activity while they are among us, and that we learn
from them how to serve them and all our brothers and sisters of creation.

In the silence, we waited. We waited, and then the Catholic priest behind me intoned, "We ask that we be good
stewards of the land . . ." and the assembly moved on, to
pray for the church, our communities, and world peace.

Once again, I had not spoken for the owls.

## The Owls and the Mentor

"I liked your letter," the thin, quavery voice told me over
the phone. I was chatting with my eighty-six-year-old mentor, an ethicist I'd had as a professor in college. He was
growing increasingly frail, but fortunately his mind, always
distinguished by creativity and vision, was still keen.

"I liked reading about the owls," he continued. Had I
written about the owls? I usually write whatever is on my
mind, and owls had been on my mind each day. Their large
feathered forms penetrated the far recesses of my imagination. Our resident owls, the great horneds and the barreds,
were in the process of nesting and laying eggs. We sometimes heard a pair at night, calling to each other in the dark.
We have a great horned owl nest a few miles from our house.
It is astonishingly large, brushy with big sticks, at the very
crown of an oak, and exposed to the elements. A great horned

owl incubating eggs during a February blizzard feels the full brunt of the wind. How big must a great gray owl's nest be? I had read that great grays that have traveled south in the winter might not nest the following spring. Our visitors aren't only hungry, but missing out on that most essential of activities for a healthy population, reproduction.

"Are they another sign of global warming?" the mentor wanted to know.

"Oh, no, no," I assured him. "They're here because their food supply up north is very low. No, this is a normal event."

But was it? In December, it seemed normal, but three months later people were taken aback by the proportions of the irruption. They were looking for explanations. One researcher had found that the meadow mouse population in his study plot in Canada was at its lowest numbers in ten years. A wet, cold spring last year had hampered reproduction, and a warm, dry fall had also killed off mice. He thought that the unfavorable weather, superimposed on a natural population low, had created the dire situation.

## The Owls as Messengers

As I write this, it is now mid-March. After a week's hiatus, when no one I knew saw any owls, I spied one yesterday in the shadows of a hedgerow, at the apex of a small pine. True to type, it was focused on the field in front of it. My husband and I viewed it in profile, seeing one yellow eye and half the white bowtie feathers of its neck. However, this time, we did not linger to savor the bird. We drove straight through, so as not to attract attention. We have learned at least that much.

In the Harry Potter books, owls are messengers, carrying notes from the Ministry of Magic to Hogwarts School, from parents to children, from students to their friends. Messages from upset parents to erring children are sometimes what are called "howlers," which scream and rant when taken from the owl and opened. I can't shake off the sense that the owls this winter have carried messages to us, but unlike Harry or Hermione, I can't simply remove the leg band and unfold a note.

In Native American lore, an owl is a harbinger of death. Owls appear sometimes as premonitions of impeding demise: "I heard the owl call my name." But death is not so much obliteration as it is a netherworld, the world below, dark, shadowy, and something less than alive.

Is that the message? That we are headed for a netherworld? For all our sakes, I pray it is not. But things are not well in the north. Polar bears are losing shelf ice, the permafrost is thawing, a world that has depended on a stable climate is unraveling. It is not so much death as it is a graying of vibrancy, a move toward being less alive.

Perhaps the owls' message is much simpler and straightforward: we're in trouble. We know that much is true.

# What Are Animals For?

It was one of those transition days. On a gray September morning, a slight mist hung on the air, as if a gauzy curtain had been dropped over the stage, signaling the end of Act One and hiding from view the preparations for Act Two. Pioneer takes on a mysterious aspect on days like this. It ceases to present itself as a straightforward little lake and assumes instead a cloak of inscrutability. Anything becomes possible.

I was out on the lake in the canoe, taking some exercise and checking out the migrating ducks that had dropped in to Pioneer for a rest and a bite to eat. I was hoping to see something exotic. Pioneer usually only attracts the most commonplace: mallards, teal, wood ducks, lesser scaup in spring. I heard a splash behind me and turned around to see two dark forms tussling in the water. I was momentarily taken aback. Black ducks? Coot? What would cause ducks to fight in the fall? Looking again, I realized I was watching not birds but long, slender forms—mink? Otters! There were river otters on Pioneer, and they were rolling about in the shallow bay, splattering water in all directions, and generally creating a ruckus.

Otters are an infrequent sight in our neck of the woods. The first I recall seeing were on the Rum River, about twenty miles west. Our family came upon them one summer afternoon as we canoed down the river. The Rum cuts through agricultural land, but its banks are shaded by box elders, and the otters had made a slide on a slope beneath the boughs. Three or four, undoubtedly a family group of cubs and their mother, were taking turns skimming down a slick, muddy run from the top of the riverbank into the water. There seemed to be no reason for doing this other than it was fun—at least, it looked fun to us.

We were charmed. How often is it that people watch animals goofing off? Wild animals are sober, industrious creatures, doing everything for a purpose, wasting not a single calorie in frivolous activity. Some evolutionary biologists claim that this is the only way to explain animal behavior. Even what looks to us like play is assigned evolutionary benefit. The sliding otters, probably siblings, or parents and children, were bonding. They were exercising large muscle groups. They were rehearsing escape strategies to employ when confronted with a predator. They couldn't have been goofing off on a nice summer day. What adaptive benefit could that wastrel activity have?

Back on Pioneer Lake, the wrestling otters—which looked to me like they were having fun—became alert to my presence. They froze, heads in midair, then dove into the lake and disappeared. I kept alert for the otters the remainder of the fall, but they appeared only that once. It was as if the mist, while obscuring most objects, had revealed them to me, and when it lifted, they evaporated as well.

Months later, on a cold, frosty, January day, they reappeared. Not the animals themselves but evidence that they had been in the area. This is how wild animals often reveal their presence—in past tense. Nature, like a cipher, seemingly prefers to speak in code. In the case of otters in winter, this is stunningly, weirdly like a visual Morse code, that is, little round paw prints followed by a long, tunnel-like indentation in the snow. Otters traverse open ground by loping then sliding, loping and sliding.

Two otters, it seemed, had traveled side by side along the eastern shore of Pioneer, right past our dock laying in winter senescence on dry land, past our neighbors, and on to the alder thicket on the north end of the lake. I could tell they had paused a moment to check out the dock; their tracks embroidered the perimeter. On the south end of the lake, the tracks trailed off toward the road. It seemed likely that the pair had crossed the road and church parking lot, moving back and forth between Pioneer and a shallow, marshy bay of South Center Lake. I wondered if that explained why I had not seen otters on Pioneer of late—they had been spending most of their time on the larger lake.

Otter young are born in late winter or early spring. I imagined my two to be a mated pair, the female growing larger with the developing cubs within her. At some point, they must look for a suitable place to raise a family. They often take over a bank burrow made by a beaver or muskrat, or hole up under a log protruding from the water.

After finding the tracks tracing the shoreline, I added a new dimension to my ski trips around the frozen lake. I began looking for suitable otter housing, eying each log, each exposed bank. Would that offer enough protection? Was this location hidden from view? Would the snowmobiles that zoomed up and down the length of Pioneer discover a nest made in that bank?

At a book signing, I mentioned the otters to a neighbor. Oh, yes, he told me. There'd been otters one time on nearby Little Lake, too. He'd seen them frolicking in a marsh one evening. Sadly, a few weeks later, he'd come upon four skinned and bloodied carcasses laid out in a row. Must have been trapped for their pelts, he'd remarked. Otter pelts must bring a pretty penny. Either that, or they'd encountered traps set for beavers. He shrugged and looked regretful. They'd been a pleasing sight, playing.

My heart froze. I hadn't considered the possibility of their being trapped. From then on, I mentioned the otters to no one.

If I had recalled Minnesota history, trapping might have been the first thing I associated with otters. These long, slinky cousins to minks and ermines have long been prized for their thick, luxurious fur. The first Europeans to live for any length of time in Minnesota were trappers, and though we tend to consider the beaver the chief focus of fur trappers' attention, river otter was, and still is, a highly valued fur-bearer. Unregulated trapping played a significant role in the loss of otters from the state's waterways.

It wasn't only trapping, though, that caused the decline of otters in the southern two-thirds of North America in the 1800s. Their downfall was hastened by the degradation of their habitat. As forests were cleared, streams became silted, and cutover riverbanks no longer provided shelter for nests. The use of the pesticides DDT and dieldrin after World War II also devastated the fish-eating mammals. These insecticides accumulate in fat tissue and concentrate higher up the food chain. Otters, as top-of-the-line predators, got hefty doses with each meal. That class of poisons was outlawed in 1973 in the United States, but in England, where it was legal until 1989, otters showed damage to their retinas, caused by dieldrin buildup in their tissues; dieldrin affects the activity of vitamin A in the body.

With these deadly poisons no longer in use and the restoration of unpolluted water and vegetated riverbanks, wildlife specialists are optimistic about the otter's future. The specialist in charge of Minnesota's furbearer program tells me that the river otter is "doing fine" in Minnesota. He bases his information on the number of pelts obtained by trappers each year. This past season, 3,208 otter pelts were registered with state officials. The estimated population is about twelve thousand individuals. In order to trap any furbearers, trappers must have a license, and each pelt sold to a buyer must be tagged by the state. There are perhaps more otters in northern Minnesota than in the southern two-thirds, doubtless because logging does not have the impact on their riverine habitat that the cleared and drained fields of agriculture do.

The devastation of the river otter population occurred all over North America, and several states now have high-profile otter reintroduction programs. New York, Indiana, and Nebraska are all engaged in campaigns to restore river habitat and water quality so that captive-bred otters can be released into their original habitat. Of course, these states do not allow the trapping of otters. They are pursuing the opposite intent. I did notice on one Web site, however, that a trappers' organization is a sponsor of New York's reintroduction effort.

Who buys otter pelts in these days of paint-throwing animal rights activists? According to the furbearer expert at the state Department of Natural Resources, the big market is in Russia and China. Representatives of those countries' fur trade come to North America to bid on pelts of all kinds—beaver, fox, coyote, mink, even skunk. At first glance, it is baffling that places like Russia and China should import furs. Both are immense northern countries, where furbearing animals once lived in abundance. Mammals from cold climates have the most luxuriant pelts, and both the Chinese and Russians traditionally wore fur. Think of the hats in *Doctor Zhivago*. But pondering more, I realize that both countries also have horrible track records in protecting their environments. Pollution is rampant and habitat degradation is widespread. So, the wealthy search in the New World for what the older civilizations have spoiled.

An otter pelt will sell for about $125, an increase in price from five years ago. In that regard, life is good for the Minnesota trapper. Overall, though, relatively few people trap anymore. In the 1940s, when the population of Minnesota was less than half what it is today, there were fifty-five thousand trappers setting lines. That number declined to twenty-five thousand in the 1960s. Today, despite a demand from the world's largest country, there are fewer than six thousand. The decline of people making a living from trapping is a reflection of many trends. Surely, societal values and the popularity of the belief that people shouldn't choose to wear fur play a part. But it is also true that we are less in contact with nature these days, as more and more people leave rural areas to live in suburbs. Like hunting and fishing, the art of trapping is not being passed on to the next generation. Trappers are concerned that this particular livelihood from the land is dying, and with it a part of our historic past. They advertise "young trapper programs" to interest children in the activity. At present, the legal age at which a child can run a trapline is eight. They'd like to see it lowered.

Notice the terms. Otters are not mere mammals, they are *furbearers*. Their skin, with its hair, has its own word, *pelt*. They fall under the jurisdiction of the department of *Natural Resources* and are "an available supply that can be drawn upon when needed," my dictionary's definition of a *resource*. And when they are "drawn upon" and killed, they are considered *harvested*, which my dictionary tells me is "the act or process of gathering a crop."

I'm not sure applying agricultural terminology to wild

animals (or plants—natural forests, when cut, are also said to be "harvested") is appropriate. It assumes a manner of husbandry that we simply don't perform. The otters brought forth young by their own efforts, not ours. In fact, given the number of obstacles we've managed to put in their way— habitat loss, pollution, urbanization—we might say they've reproduced in spite of us. Who is the owner of this resource who can rightfully claim the profit when money changes hands?

We don't have a good answer to this question. If the answer is—and even this is a stretch for me—that we, the people, own our natural resources, then why do a few people earn money selling our collectively owned resources to wealthy Chinese? It's an unsettling picture, imagining a silky, dark fur grown in the cutover woods of the Arrowhead region gracing a coat worn by a person striding down the streets of Shanghai.

So let's try again. Who is the owner of these resources? Perhaps the fault lies in our language. The words we have to denote a relationship between people and wild animals is one of ownership, an understanding that in these times, when many wild animal populations are pressed to the wall, is no longer useful. We think only as far as our words allow us, and in truth they are wholly inadequate. This inadequacy is revealed when we ask the questions of ownership: who planted? Who bought? Who nurtured?

The animals that we *own* are those we have domesticated. Tame, docile pets, like cats and dogs, mild-mannered cattle, tractable horses. When a domestic animal shows any wildness, like an unbreakable horse, or an untrainable pit bull, we back off from ownership—at least, the rights of ownership lessen—and the dog that has proved a menace to others may well be put down.

Annie Dillard writes of "owning" a pet goldfish, which she conditioned, through raps on the side of its aquarium, to rise to the expectation of fish flakes. But ownership, even of a fish, made her wary. To her, animals somehow have a standing that precludes being owned.

Where does this sense of ownership spring from? Is it a legacy from the Bible, particularly the Genesis creation story? Some people love to seize on the passage when God bestows "dominion" over other animals on the human beings. However, a careful reading of the story reveals no type of ownership as we understand it in a free trade society. Indeed, a footnote in my Bible points out that the "dominion" is limited, benevolent, and peaceful, as shown by the edict that people eat only plants. It would seem more likely that those who use the Bible to back up their actions have seized a passage that suits them and molded it to their desire. Not the first time that's been done.

Mulling all this over, I recall that first image of the pair of otters rolling about in the water. What a deceptively light-hearted veneer to the dark, shadowy relationship we maintain with the furbearers.

An otter's home range is large, as befitting a top-of-the-food-chain predator. Biologists estimate that families travel about three to ten miles in a season, but individuals have been known to move fifty to sixty miles in a year. When otters have been trapped out of a river system, as has happened in the lower St. Croix River, others have repopulated the unoccupied habitat from the upper reaches of the river. When I learned this, I was no longer uneasy that the otter presence on Pioneer waxed and waned. The animals were like spooks, appearing as movement out of the corner of my eye, or visible only as tracings in the snow. Like ghosts, they became the topic of hearsay. My sister-in-law reported coming upon one while she walked her dog near the little bay of South Center Lake. Friends from church caught a glimpse by their shoreline. I happened on one on a run around the lake—a shy, slinky sylph who vanished even as I recognized it.

The presence of the otters enlivened my sense of the lake. Just knowing they were out there made the austere winter aspect of the ice seem less barren and more like a screen, concealing the roiling variety of unseen creation. The otters became ambassadors of the wild underbelly of Pioneer Lake. Life in Center City—life anywhere in our well-domesticated land—can seem tame and prosaic. The intermittent presence of the otters served as witness that the appearance of domesticity was superficial only.

The thin snow cover of the dry winter had vanished, but Pioneer was still iced over at the end of March, the time when otter young are born. One afternoon, I pulled on rubber boots and headed down to the ice, thinking to collect pussy willows as a bouquet for the dinner table. I wanted one more time on the ice before it broke up, and its surface was growing dark in color, a sign that it was going. We had been away on vacation and I thought the ice might tell me what I had missed when I was gone. There was a thin gap between the shoreline and the ice sheet. I sunk several inches in slush as I stepped onto the lake and decided it would be best to stay in near shore. Far off, several geese, arriving too early for open water, honked companionably.

There were no willows in flower. I would have to make do with hothouse daisies. But several hundred yards ahead on the ice, I saw something that looked like a stone. When I reached it, I saw it was the skull of some kind of weasel; at first glance, I was pretty sure, an otter. The head had been severed from the body and the skin removed. Evidently, the skull was not worth anything.

Except to me. I picked it up and took it home. I intend to clean it up and keep it on my desk. Each time I see it, I'll ask myself this question: what are animals for?

# Ever Living Fire

The moon waxed full the second week in April. The night was illuminated with such brilliance that at times I could not sleep and, instead, wandered the half-lit house, looking out over a yard drenched in moonlight. This was the first full moon after the vernal equinox, the celestial event that signaled the start of a new year for the ancient Hebrews. I like the idea of beginning a new year with the coming of spring. Beginnings are abundant in March and April, much more so than in January. After a natural pause at the end of winter, leaves begin to form on trees, migratory birds arrive to start their breeding season, and other animals come out of hibernation to resume their lives.

This first full moon after the vernal equinox marks the beginning of the Hebrew month of Nisan and the start of the Jewish Passover, a celebration of freedom from the bonds of slavery. Passover begins at sundown, just as the full moon is rising.

On Monday in the second week in April, I watched it ascend, round and creamy over the bare, colorless soybean field to our east. It was a vision of splendor in a spring sky still rosy with the setting sun. Days quickly lengthen around the vernal equinox. By April, there is enough light in the evening for a walk around the lake after supper, or for some scratching in the garden.

Northerners become deliriously happy with the lengthening days. The apparent death of nature, caused by the short days and weakened sun, now appears as an illusion. Life has rebounded robustly. We have renewed reason to anticipate a green world and the sweetness of summer. In resonance with this natural heartbeat, the Passover also celebrates a deliverance from death. In the Exodus, the central, defining event of Judaism, the angel of death recognizes the blood of sacrifice on the door frame of each Jewish house and passes over it, sparing the first-born son of each family. When I was a child and heard this story in Sunday school, the angel of death assumed in my mind's eye a dark and fearsome form. I imagined it as a shadowy figure, perhaps with a staff, or a wand, like the dark fairy in *Sleeping Beauty*. It cast its shade on each door, bestowing death on some families and life on others. But as an adult, I find it difficult to recognize the angel of death in its various forms. I often cannot discern whether it stands in shadow or moonlight.

The angel of death paused over Pioneer Lake this spring. The very day of the Passover moon the ice that had capped the lake since November broke up, revealing silent mayhem. Pale, bloated bodies of dead fish floated belly up on its surface. The lake had suffered a phenomenon known to limnologists as winterkill. At the shore, I gazed at a dead bass, its eyes opaque, its sheen vanished. Nearby, a bleached body of a leopard frog hung motionless and upright in the water, gently swaying with the ripples. Another lay on the mucky bottom. Both were close to where I had emptied a bucket of live, squirmy frogs in November after rescuing them from where they had fallen into a window well of the house. A piscine odor of rot permeated the chilly air.

Usually, the day the ice goes out is a day of celebration. I feel ecstatic looking at the newly released water, sparkling in the sunlight. Suddenly, the world looks bluer and more luminous, as the lake's surface reflects the light and color of the sky. But this year, the ice retreated slowly, and while I took in the dead bodies and the stench, most of the lake remained under the pall of gray, decaying ice. It was both unsettling and fascinating.

A lake experiences winterkill when the organisms living under its ice use up most of the oxygen dissolved in its waters. Once a lake freezes in the fall, oxygen from the atmosphere cannot replenish the supply in the lake. The fish, frogs, turtles, bacteria, and other life forms that overwinter in the lake have a finite amount to last until spring. Pioneer has several features that make it a prime candidate to deplete its oxygen. Its shallow basin holds relatively little water, and so a proportionately smaller amount of oxygen. The abundance of detritus—decaying plant and algal material— also contributes to an oxygen dearth. Bacteria using oxygen are at work breaking down the detritus, and they compete with the larger creatures for the precious gas.

Not everything dies in a winterkilled lake. Usually, some creatures manage to escape the fate of the majority. The small, the inactive, those able to eke by on very little oxygen, hang on until ice-out, when the great store of atmospheric oxygen once more becomes available. Bullheads especially seem to do well at low oxygen levels, probably because they are equipped with an internal "swim bladder" connected to their gut, their own personal reservoir of oxygen.

The residents in Pioneer lead a perilous life. The ecosystem has run low on oxygen several times in the thirteen winters we've lived on its shores. Just three years ago, the DNR judged it severely winterkilled and caught only thirty-eight fish, most of them bullheads, in trap nets set in July the following summer. The fish population had only three years to build up before dying off again.

Still, on the day of ice-out, I had trouble believing that the lake, newly released from the bondage of the ice, held less life than it had in November. This was especially so because of the squawks and screeches emanating from its surface. As the ice began to give way, the sheet receding from shore, hundreds of ring-billed gulls descended. Attracted by the dead fish and the promise of an easy meal, they flocked to the feast. Although they are attractive birds, gulls are neither dainty nor refined. Twenty feet from shore, on the crumbling ice, a trio battled over a small, limp bullhead. Screaming, jeering, charging, and posturing, they pulled it this way and that. Their snowy silhouettes bobbed and jerked in the melee. Similar skirmishes were occurring all over the ice. Off shore in open water, hundreds of gulls rested on the surface, or wheeled overhead, shrieking. I felt as if I had been invited to a rowdy party where the music of the band was drowned out by the din of the revelers.

The gulls were not the only ones bent on transforming death into life. Off in the distance on a quiet section of the lake, a loon reposed serenely. I might be tempted to carry the party metaphor further and label the solitary loon a wallflower, but loons are too elegant for that word. As I watched, the sleek bird ducked beneath the surface and emerged with a fish—dead, I judged, from its listlessness. The loon repositioned the prey in its bill, then swallowed.

A raft of migratory ducks, decked out in bright breeding plumage, hung out at the edge of the alder island in the northern bay of Pioneer. Redheads with rusty domes, ring-necked drakes with variegated bills, and buffleheads flashing a striking black-and-white form all fall into the category of diving ducks—those that rely on fish for a major portion of their diet. These weary travelers, too, benefited from the catastrophe of the winterkill.

*Oikos,* the Greeks called it, the word at the root of *ecosystem,* this great house of the world, a house where everything is recycled and nothing is wasted. Life fades into death and death springs to life in the guts of the gulls and the loon and the ducks. Who or what is the angel of death here? The recorder of the Exodus muddies the waters in his answer: in the Bible, the angel of death is the Lord.

I was standing by my kitchen window a few days later, on Good Friday morning, the day Christians commemorate the crucifixion of Jesus. I was watching my daughters dye eggs when the thud of a large-bodied bird hitting the pane grabbed my attention. In a split second I recognized the bold markings of a flicker, breathed a sigh of relief that it hadn't broken the window—the impact had been that forceful—and looked out to see where it had landed. Expecting to find a lifeless mound of feathers, I instead watched as a Cooper's hawk swooped in and nailed the dazed flicker in midair. Feathers exploded, and as I gasped, the hawk hauled the flicker off to the woods and disappeared from sight.

I expect death on Good Friday. On that day of all days, it should be unequivocal. Even so, I wasn't sure of what I had seen. April is the nesting season for Cooper's hawks, and my angel of death, a male, was probably feeding a mate confined to a nest, incubating eggs. The hawk dies if it cannot kill songbirds. The flicker had died so that the hawk might live.

As Paul Gruchow writes in his book *Grass Roots,* "death is nothing if not discrete," or perhaps he meant to say "discreet," although neither word gives the whole picture.

Instead, I would suggest that *amorphous* is what death is— lacking discernible limit or form. At any given moment, we are both living and dying. How can we tell if the tide has turned, and life is ebbing and not flowing? And who are we to say that this is true death and not, rather, life in disguise, transferring from one form to another?

Every summer I help staff the Audubon booth at the state fair for a day. Invariably, visitors will drop by to tell me about a Cooper's hawk that has been persisting in their yards, preying on songbirds at their feeders. "What should we do?" they will ask. What is the answer to predation? Having witnessed the bloody act myself, I empathize with their consternation. It seems treacherous to lure orioles and cardinals to my yard, only to serve them on a platter to a Cooper's hawk. "Well," I say, fingering the National Audubon badge pinned to my collar, "Cooper's hawks are native birds, and they have to eat, too."

I, myself, have taken down my birdfeeders.

One week after Good Friday, I was out on my daily run on a county road. It was now Easter, a cheerful season, and I was enjoying the sunshine at midday, a mile and a half from the house. Suddenly, a flicker took flight from the roadside and lumbered heavily to a nearby tree. "My first flicker," I thought, "since The Murder."

Before I could reflect on a world that seemed able to effortlessly replenish the flicker supply, another bird vied for my attention. Rising swiftly from the ditch was a Cooper's hawk (ye gods, not again), clutching a second flicker in its talons, probably the mate of the one in the tree. The hawk crossed the road in front of me and disappeared into a shelterbelt of Scotch pine, the flicker emitting weak distress calls.

This time, a windowpane did not separate me from the action. "I'm going to rescue that flicker," I told myself. "I'll find it and wrap it in my shirt and take it to a wildlife rehabilitator." Hadn't I just read in the morning paper that northern flickers were on the decline in Minnesota? I took off in hot pursuit.

On hands and knees under the Scotch pines, I tried to locate the cry of the wounded bird, but all was silent in the shelterbelt. A farmer was plowing a field nearby, and gulls drawn to the upturned earth circled overhead, piping at a pitch nearly that of the flicker's. I became confused. How could the Cooper's hawk hide? What cries were the gulls and what was the flicker? Maybe the hawk had only appeared to seek out the shelterbelt and was really off in the woods. I returned to the road.

Back home, I wondered why I had so readily taken the part of the flicker and not concerned myself with the fate of the Cooper's hawk. As a zoologist, I intellectually understand predation, and I know young hawks experience many missed opportunities while honing the skills they need to successfully capture dinner. Part of my response can be explained as the human tendency to cheer for the underdog. If I had recently seen a video of an immature hawk learning to catch prey, I would probably have been more sympathetic to the raptor's needs. The cries of the doomed flicker caught my attention, though. They were far more dramatic than hunger.

Humans, the most rapacious of predators, incongruously identify with prey animals. It is not merely that we hide from ourselves the fact that we are predators of a high degree, with our neatly wrapped packages of beef and pork in the grocery store and our refined use of the language, substituting *juice* for *blood*, and *meat* for *muscle, arteries,* and *tendons.* If we were to be more blatant about our status as predators, about the slaughter of animals for our table, would we sympathize more with other predators? I doubt it.

Empathy with the prey probably resides in our deepest, instinctive fears. We all know what it feels like to be chased. In nightmares, we may know the terror of being caught. When I first learned that grizzly bears stalk humans for miles before an attack, it took no effort for me to imagine myself as a deer or a rabbit. Hikes in grizzly territory became unappealing. Predation distresses me. I am too much in love with the world. I witness the remains of a downy baby bluebird chewed up by a red squirrel, or a northern pike pulling a duckling under, and rebel at rules that are not to my liking. The law of ecology is efficient, but nonnegotiable. The contract is written in blood. If you want to live, you eat other living things. Only green plants are exempt.

I long for the day when I am at home in this world of blood and glory, when I can admire a Cooper's hawk at its finest, when the pang of loss at the death of a flicker does not consume me. Serene equanimity is the domain of sages, and I want to be numbered in their ranks.

It is now a month beyond the first full moon of the vernal equinox. In the intervening weeks, the moon has been whittled to a small sliver, gone out, and waxed full again. Once more I am restlessly wandering the house at night. I have taken to reading. I sit in a darkened room with a single pool of light from a table lamp, in a chair where I can see the shimmer of moonlight on Pioneer's water. This month I am rereading Annie Dillard's *Pilgrim at Tinker Creek*, a good companion in the quiet of the night. Its opening quote by Heraclitus returns to me whenever I mull over the vulnerability of the songbirds at my feeder and the imminent return of the Cooper's hawk: "It ever was, and is, and shall be, ever-living Fire, in measures being kindled and in measures going out."

# Winged Wonder

One chilly April morning, I glanced out the window to see a brownish butterfly clinging to one of the fuzzy flowers of our red maple. A spring wind tossed the branches, and the butterfly, intent on extracting whatever it could from such a spare flower, rode the undulating perch like a small boat in high seas. It seemed incredible to me that an adult butterfly would be on the wing so early in the season, that its heart would beat, that its muscles contract on so cool a day. The spring was still quite young. Our woods were naked, only the maples and box elder showing any signs of life. There were lingering traces of snow, in fact, in the shaded areas of the yard.

I ran to get my field guide to butterflies. I had glimpsed a broad orange band on the upper wings and knew I could identify it, given a photo. I whipped through the first part of the guide: not a swallowtail, not a white or sulphur, not a blue. I slowed down when I got to the section depicting medium-sized insects with irregular wing edges and found it: Milbert's tortoiseshell. I'd scribbled in the margins of its page that I'd seen one last fall on September 20, feeding on asters.

Butterflies are engaging creatures. Most are beautiful, some stunningly so. Their delicacy and ephemerality incite wonder and regard. How is it possible that nature, which can be so brutal and brash, makes room for creatures so wispy

and insubstantial? Their common names have a charming,
elfin quality: checkerspots, commas, question marks, skip-
pers, pearly eyes, dusky wings, wood nymphs. I sometimes
think that the collectors who named them had elfin qualities
as well. I imagine them as wispy characters, perhaps with
hair sprouting from their ears, bending over trays of moth-
balled specimens, totally immersed in a curatorial world.

Milbert's tortoiseshell has all the gossamer butterfly
appeal. With a wingspan of just over two inches, it is considered a medium-sized butterfly. Broad orange bands follow the curve of its wings, giving rise to an alternative name,
fire-rim tortoiseshell. Electric blue spots dot the wing margins. Like monarchs, and fritillaries, it is a brush-footed butterfly, family Nymphalidae. The first pair of its six legs is
shortened and covered with fine hairs. Nymphalids tend to
be active flyers, seen flitting from flower to flower, promi-
nent features of a summer landscape.

As a graduate student, I took a field entomology course
one summer at the university's biological research station
in Itasca State Park. As part of the course requirement, I made
a small insect collection that included the most common
moths and butterflies: a monarch, a tiger swallowtail, a cab-
bage white (the ones that lay their eggs on broccoli), a tiny
Eastern blue.

In biology, identification of unknown organisms often
uses a dichotomous key, an elaborate set of pairs of choices,
from which you select for smaller and smaller details. The
first choice in the key to the lepidoptera, the butterflies and
moths, for example, is "wings present and well-developed"
or "wings absent," and you choose whichever best applies
to the organism under your scrutiny. A series of choices elim-
inates possibilities until the one remaining is the name of
the organism. The entomology textbook in my Itasca course

own key, which is what we used for identifi-
catch. Sadly, it only ID'd the insects down to
the handsome, large black-and-yellow swal-
ample, was merely identified as Papilionidae.
in other courses of study, I was accustomed to being able to
identify every organism to a species level, and to know the
common name. The insect world is so vast, tens of millions
of species, most of them as yet not identified, that even the
insects of the state park couldn't be mastered in a short six-
week course. This was an unsatisfying way to know an animal. One can hardly become acquainted with the life of a
butterfly if one doesn't know its name. Intimacy begins in
all cases with a name, and my main interest in the course
was to become conversant with the insect world, as I was
with birds.

Twenty-five years later, I have recently acquired a very
good visually oriented field guide that is specific to the
northern woods of Minnesota, not exactly my home in Chisago County but close enough. It covers most of Pioneer
Lake's resident lepidopterans and shows photos and lists
common names. The photographs are clear and brightly
colored, and each entry has ample natural history information. My interest has reawakened, and I have increased my
efforts to become acquainted with small, colorful, winged
animals.

Most butterflies overwinter as eggs, caterpillars, or chrys-
alises. A few, like the monarch, deal with potentially fatal
temperatures by migrating. But Milbert's tortoiseshell is one
of a handful of species in Minnesota that survive the winter
as adults. Consequently, it is considered a long-lived butterfly. The adult form can live nine to ten months. Most adult
butterfly life spans are measured in days. The Milbert's tortoiseshell I'd seen in September was very possibly newly

hatched. The Milbert's has two broods of caterpillars each year, with eggs laid soon after adults emerge from the winter and again in midsummer. They can be seen on the wing from mid-June through mid-August, and again in early September to early May (with time-out for hibernation.) As the weather cools and days grow short in the fall, the adults seek out protected hibernacula, under the loose bark of decaying trees, in hollow stumps, even in old barns or outbuildings. Often many will congregate together, packed, as one naturalist describes it, "like bluebirds in a nestbox."

Yet in Minnesota, not even the best-protected site can keep the butterflies from experiencing temperatures below freezing. With body fluid mainly comprising water, just like us, and no ability to generate a lot of heat, unlike us, these animals face the danger of freezing. Ice crystals can act as tiny spears, puncturing cell membranes and other structures, causing extensive damage and death. We so seldom consider how animals, other than those so obvious like farm animals or family pets, make it through the winter, and yet winter comprises the longest season of the year.

Northern butterflies that overwinter as adults solve the problem of water in solid state by making glycerol, or some other kind of alcohol, in the fall. Glycerol, a ubiquitous compound that is used by humans as a sweetener in foods and toothpaste, as an emollient in cosmetics and lotions, and in myriad other products including chemical antifreezes, acts as a natural antifreeze in a butterfly's body and hinders the formation of ice crystals. The insect's blood is loaded with glycerol as it spends the winter in a type of dormancy.

As soon as spring temperatures warm the hibernaculum, adults are set to fly. They emerge somewhat paler than they were in the fall and perhaps a bit tattered by a long winter, but vigorous enough to feed and mate and leave eggs that begin the cycle again. Like mourning cloaks, commas, and question marks, they are the first butterflies that appear, signaling the coming of spring.

Soon after I spotted the Milbert's tortoiseshell on the red maple, spring burst open. With the coming of warm weather, we eagerly began our yard and garden cleanup, preparing for the new growing season. One Saturday at lunch, after a morning spent happily grubbing about, removing mulch, turning over garden box soil, and planting cool-weather seeds, Tom remarked, "A job well done!" He'd been in the backyard, laying a walkway down to the lake. "I pulled up a ton of nasty nettles!" he told me, and rolled up a sleeve to display a rather inflamed right forearm.

I looked at him over my soup and said, "You know, I was just reading last week that Milbert's tortoiseshell lays its eggs exclusively on nettle."

"On stinging nettle?" he wanted to know.

"Yes, what other kind of nettle is there? *Utica.*" I was referring to the genus name, which Tom and I had both learned in a botany course.

"You just can't win," he replied, looking somewhat vexed.

Stinging nettle is the sole host for the eggs of the lovely Milbert's. Females lay pale green eggs in clusters numbering up to nine hundred on the underside of the plant's leaves. Young caterpillars emerge and remain together on the host, enclosed in a silky, communal web that protects them from predators and may also serve to keep the growing caterpillars somewhat warm. It pleases me that this problematic plant, such a bane to gardeners, can produce something beautiful. It really proves the saying that a weed is merely a plant out of place.

I give nettle a wide berth when weeding my garden. The leaves contain little stinging hairs that cause human skin to burn like crazy when it contacts them. The chemicals causing such irritation are believed to be histamine and acetylcholine. Each sting hair on a nettle leaf has a sharp-pointed tip, the opening to a slender tube that leads to a fluid-filled sac in the leaf. When a hair is touched, the tip bends, penetrates the skin, and results in pressure put on the sac to release the irritants into the skin of the passerby. I always remove nettle from my garden, but I use gloves and carefully grasp the plant at its very base, where the stinging hairs seem to be absent. Even so, I sometimes get a burn through the cotton fabric of the fingertips. I put this plant in the same category as I do meadow mice in my kitchen: perfectly acceptable, even desirable. But not in this particular place.

Some butterfly gardeners, however, actually plant nettle by choice. Other beautiful butterflies lay their eggs on nettle: the showy red admiral; the orange, ruffly Eastern comma; question marks; and the rare satyr comma. We have enough leeway in our yard to have both cultivated and uncultivated portions. I'll continue to yank it from my vegetable boxes, but it can flourish and host baby caterpillars in the greater portion of the yard we keep au naturel.

How my world has opened up, thanks to my butterfly guide! I now see Milbert's tortoiseshells all over, their orange-and-brown wings gaily hovering over cultivated garden blooms and roadside wildflowers. Butterflies have been hard hit by the widespread use of pesticides in the second half of the twentieth century. They were once a common feature of a sunny summer day. We see many more species and individuals at our cabin in northern Wisconsin in remote, cut-over woods than we do here on the shore of Pioneer Lake, surrounded as we are by suburban lawns and agricultural fields. Whenever I encounter a number of butterflies, when I'm hiking or on a trip, I know that there's not extensive chemical use in the area. Butterflies are a mark of environmental health.

I remember when I first became caught up in the study of animals, like the delicate butterflies. It was in the spring of my freshman year at college, nearly thirty-five years ago. Butterflies must have been on the wing then, just as they are on the breezy May day on which I write this essay so many years later. In those early days of study, I was just beginning to understand that the more I knew, the more I realized how little I really understood. Facts just deepened the mystery of life. Possessing detailed knowledge of nature made me euphoric. Even the notoriously dry study of taxonomy, the laborious task of memorizing genus and species names, delighted me. I swear the feeling was closely akin to that of being in love.

One day I sat in the cafeteria, pouring over my zoology text, reviewing one last time before the final exam the characteristics and lineage of the phylum Arthropoda. It is the big one in the animal kingdom, encompassing crustaceans, spiders, millipedes, horseshoe crabs, centipedes, and all the myriad insects, including butterflies. I memorized these facts: arthropods have external skeletons, compound eyes, jointed legs—that's what the name means—a segmented body plan (like earthworms), and an open circulatory system with a heart and blood vessels and hemolymph, their version of blood. My companion, a religion major, watched me and remarked, "I'd rather not know the science behind some things. It ruins my sense of wonder."

I lifted my bleary eyes from the page momentarily, ran his comment through my mind so filled with facts, considered a biosphere filled with billions of tiny beating butterfly hearts, and said, with amazement, "Really?"

# The Rites of Spring

The Lutherans worshiping in the yellow brick church at the southern end of Pioneer Lake don't distinguish between low and high worship. It is true that some services are fancier than others, but we have lost the language that distinguishes the festive from the more mundane. Through transfer from Europe to the New World, through neglect, through downright hostility to our origins in the Roman Catholic Church, we have lost the words that helped us articulate what we're about each Sunday.

Perhaps if we had retained them, we could better characterize the nature of spring. Just as a quiet, subdued low mass ushers in a Sunday morning, so spring begins on a subtle note, as if too much gaudy display would overwhelm our winter-weary selves. There is such a marked contrast between early spring and what happens in my birthday month, May, that I have taken to thinking about the phenomenon as "low spring" and "high spring," in the same way that others talk about "low mass" and "high mass."

At low mass, the service is spoken, not sung, by a single officiate, the priest. But my American Heritage dictionary also gives this definition of *low*: staying in hiding, biding one's time. So lowly does spring begin that I am hard-pressed to mark its first day. Late in February or early March, I'll awake one night in the dark to hear that the wind rattling the porch screens has changed. It will howl in from the south, thumping on the porch door. It will no longer cause the bare branches of the box elder tree on the north side of the house to scratch against the bedroom window. I'll think of those childhood picture book illustrations of a big, blustery, bluish face puffing and puffing, little swirls emanating from the pursed lips, pushing children down a country lane, their coats and skirts awhirl. I'll start to anticipate wet, March snows, not the dry, cutting crystals of winter. Fierce as it may seem, the blustery wind ushers in the tenderest time of year. The snow melts, the ice on Pioneer Lake breaks up, and the most daring creatures, those that appear to act only on faith, prepare for the coming summer.

The first birds to arrive from southern wintering grounds are horned larks. I begin to search for them in late February, after a warming sun has rolled back the snow cover on agricultural fields and the brown earth lies exposed. The presence of larks is as subtle as the change in the wind. You may see a rise and a flutter of winged creatures far off in the distance. Perhaps a single bird is startled from the verge of a gravel road, and you catch sight of bold, black markings on its face before it flies off. Because spring comes in fits and starts, horned larks brave blizzards, when snow will once more obscure the fields that yield their sustenance. They risk being caught in a cold snap that tests their ability to keep warm. They are the avian equivalent of early crocuses. They dare the winter to end.

Larks will not come to a bird feeder or sing loudly from an exposed perch. In these early days, they do not proclaim any patch of earth as theirs. They are merely out in the fields, just this side of the horizon, moving north with the spring. They are the promise that this winter is over. They will leave for the far north before the first flowers bloom.

Horned larks were not part of my childhood, however, which was lived out on the edge of a marsh. For me, the true presence of spring is marked by the return of red-winged blackbirds. Red-winged blackbirds reach the marshes of Chisago County some time in mid-March, almost always before the ice goes off the lakes. Their favorite perches, cattails, are dead and broken, rustling dryly in the March gales, anchored to ice in the still-frozen marsh. Nonetheless, the male blackbirds have already decided which territories to defend. Their cheery "konk-a-ree" song resonates over the straw-colored marsh grasses, and their scarlet epaulets, which they puff out in splendor, are brilliant under the weak sunlight. The mood is expectant as they wait for their ladies to return.

Often they are joined by other new arrivals. Canada geese are notable for appearing before the lakes open. I have often seen a pair standing on the ice of a small pond, dignified and elegant as always, but looking as if they have nothing to do. Decked out in black-and-white feathers, they've arrived in formal dress several days too early for the party.

The first flower of a Minnesota spring is equally low profile. It is the bloom of the red maple, *Acer rubra*. A red maple grows just beyond the window near my writing table, and I keep a close eye on it throughout the year. The flowers begin as swollen, vermilion buds on the tips of the slender wands of branches. Viewed from the distance, the profuse buds seem to swathe the tree in rosy gauze. This happens while the world is still wintry, and sometimes I awake to find wet, heavy snow clinging to the bud-laden branches. Buds progress leisurely to full-blown flowers, but one day I will notice that they have broken open and stamens have emerged. The flowers, structured for wind pollination, have no petals and are less red than the buds. The long, extruding stamens are green and soften the branches with a fuzzy aspect, like tiny bottlebrushes. My neighbor's honeybees, those that come out prematurely, hover about, attracted to the pollen.

The red maple awakens to the new season before the frost leaves the ground. Frost in Minnesota extends several feet into the earth, and before it thaws, water is frozen and cannot be tapped by the tree. Nights in March can be very cold, below zero, and the tree is drawing its energy for its venture into spring from reserves of sugar it stockpiled last summer. Like a gutsy investor, it spends its capital to reap profits later on.

The momentous changes of spring creep in, in increments, in the daily rotation of the earth, in the smallest changes in the planet's position with respect to the sun. Not showy, not noisy, without flash or color, they appear as the last snows still cover the land. They are quietly bold. They are always pushing the envelope. We can learn something from nature moving into spring: do what you've got to do. Be daring and fearless. The future belongs to those who can read the signs of change.

Easter is considered a moveable feast in the parlance of Christianity and is not assigned a fixed date like Christmas. It falls on the first Sunday after the first full moon of the vernal equinox, sometime between March 21 and April 22. In Minnesota it is almost always celebrated during this first, tender spring of chilly air and subtlety. It never conforms to the Hollywood stereotype of bright blooms and Easter bonnets and ladies strolling about with parasols.

"How I miss a southern Easter!" a minister's wife once remarked to me in her soft Texas drawl. We were gazing out together on Easter morning as a light snow fell over the soggy grass and bare trees in the church cemetery. I had recently returned from a few days in Louisiana, so I knew what she meant: the perfume of hyacinths, the lushness of green leaves, and the hot pink of azaleas. I had found it shockingly lavish. I like my Easters early, monotone, and tender, as if the world has just woken up, with sleep still in its eyes, ready to be startled into wonder. Then it seems possible that something new is truly in the offing.

I attended my first Roman Catholic High Mass away from home, on Christmas Day. The service was held in the cathedral in Freiburg, Germany, a Gothic behemoth of a building that hunkered down in the central square of the city and brought to mind images of dinosaurs and dragons and other ancient creatures. The interior of the hulking monster was cavernous, a sanctuary darkened with the soot of a thousand years, illuminated by the half-light of bejeweled windows of scarlet and sapphire glass. The minister—he must have been a bishop because he wore a miter like that of the chess piece—donned a brilliant, buttercup yellow cape at the beginning of the service and chanted the Christmas Gospel from John in a rich, baritone voice. Clouds of musky incense scented the air. In the balcony, a small orchestra and chorus sang Mozart, interspersed by the growl of the pipe organ and the singing congregation. It was standing room only on Christmas Day, and the opening hymn, "Adeste Fideles," was glorious and deafening. I had never before heard a thousand voices singing.

And then, one day in May, I stood on my own porch and listened. The din emanating from the woods assaulted my ears. Chief among the noisemakers were the Tennessee warblers who have a reputation as loudmouths. My bird guide clocks them at six to nine songs per minute. This tendency to chatter, coupled with volume, gives the impression that the Tennessees are everywhere. But it wasn't only Tennessee warblers making a racket. Concentrating, I could hear a number of other warblers singing simultaneously from various parts of the woods. I also saw movement in the trees—my porch is on the second story, eye-level with the canopy—and with my binoculars, I began to pick out an amazing array of birds.

I was in the middle of a mixed flock of wood warblers, small colorful, active birds that migrate through Minnesota in mid-May. Warblers are the darlings of the birdwatcher. Small and delicate, they are feathered in brilliant color: redstarts with sooty backs and apricot splotches on their tails and wings; Blackburnians sporting tangerine throats that seem to glow; Wilsons with yellow underneath and jaunty black caps. About twenty-eight species, all wonderfully intricate and different, move through Chisago County each spring, each with a characteristic song and a specific way of mincing about in the treetops. Many species prefer hanging out in the upper reaches of the canopy, so that birdwatchers inclined to observe them develop a condition known as "warbler neck."

The warbler season had begun, as always, with the sighting of the first yellow-rumped warbler in early April. Yellow-rumps overwinter in the southern United States, unlike most warblers that fly to Central America, and so return to us fairly soon after the snow melts. So named for the bright lemony patches at the base of their tails, yellow-rumps show up when the leaves are still tiny, promising knots on the branches of trees and shrubs. We saw dozens of them in April. They clustered on trees extending over the water by the shore of Pioneer, adorning the branches like small, agitated leaves. Singing their weak, soft warble, they fluttered back and forth from their perches, snapping up the first insects that hovered over the water. They seemed to be everywhere the day we put in the dock, filling the air with movement and the soft whir of feathers.

Now, in May, a few remained in our yard. I could hear them on the edge of the meadow, but I focused instead on the newcomers. Far off I could hear the buzzy song of black-throated green warblers: "Trees, trees, murmuring trees!" they rasped. Then came the piping boast of a chestnut-sided warbler: "Sweet, sweet, sweet, I'll switch youoooo!" Or maybe he said, in friendlier fashion, "Pleased, pleased, pleased to meetcha!" I listened carefully, because I have been known to confuse a chestnut-sided with a yellow warbler, who sings, "Sweet, sweet, sweet, you're so sweet."

In the noisy flock were nonwarblers, too. I saw several species of vireos, also arrived from the tropics: a rose-breasted grosbeak (which birdwatchers identify as sounding like "a robin in a hurry"—or a robin who's had voice lessons) and a scarlet tanager ("a robin with a sore throat"). (Note that the ubiquitous robin is the standard, although even robins can stump birders.)

A word about bird talk: ornithology students, when first learning territorial songs, adopt tricks to help remember the songs. Field guides often mention these tricks. White-throated sparrows call for "Old Sam Peabody, Peabody, Peabody," or maybe they say, "Pure, sweet, Canada, Canada, Canada!" (Alternatively, they have been heard to whistle the opening notes of Dvorak's "New World Symphony," and that is not a coincidence: the Czech composer wrote his melody after hearing the birds while visiting Iowa.) Song sparrows constantly nag, "Maids, maids, maids, put on your teakettle, -ettle, -ettle," and eastern towhees are forever urging us to "Drink your tea!" Amazingly, all the birds speak English.

Having learned these tricks, I hear bird voices now whenever the songsters are around. Everywhere I walk in high spring I hear birds "talking" to me.

Over the course of two hours, while the flock remained in the vicinity, I heard and saw eleven species of warblers, and on the next day I added two more. Almost all had migrated two thousand miles from Central America. Even in the best of times, these northward migrations are a marvel. In our times, the loss of winter habitat, the patchwork logging of breeding grounds, and the paved and altered surface of cities and towns makes their journey even more perilous. Their presence among us is miraculous.

I left the porch after awhile and walked the path through the woods in search of a few less common birds that I had heard but not seen. In mid-May, the leaves are fully out. Their canopy over my head formed a frilly, verdant ceiling. At my feet spread a carpet of common violets, and the air was fragrant with their sweet scent. It rose as incense into the humid air, and I thought, color, music, movement, scent: high spring in Minnesota.

# The Nest Box War

At the edge of our meadow rising up from Pioneer Lake, we have placed bluebird boxes, designed to attract the cheery sapphire birds to our yard. There is nothing lovelier on a summer day than to be in the presence of these beauties. "Bluebirds carry the sky on their backs," Thoreau writes, and I think of this every time a male bluebird flies by.

Bluebirds are cavity nesters, a group of birds whose populations have been declining for decades, for want of nest sites. Artificial boxes are intended to substitute for natural nest sites. In the past, cavity-nesting birds sought out woodpecker holes carved out of dead snags and, since the introduction of agriculture, holes in wooden fence posts, to serve as nest sites. However, with increasing human presence, dead trees are seldom allowed to stand; we lost one such tree, a cottonwood, a few years ago from the southeastern shore of Pioneer, a tree that had harbored a pair of nesting tree swallows, when the county took it down to tidy up a construction zone. And thin metal fence posts have replaced the old wooden ones in demarcating farm fields.

The birds have taken to the boxes with enthusiasm. Although bluebirds were the original target for the help, other cavity nesters also make use of the planned community. This summer we have bluebirds in one box, a chickadee pair in another, and a pugnacious little house wren in a third. Over the years, we have frequently played landlord to tree swallows as well, which flash about the yard in their iridescent teal-blue plumage, all of these native songbirds, which we are happy to host.

But another species, highly adaptable, has also benefited greatly from the boxes: the house sparrow. House sparrows are drab birds with a nonmelodic "cheep" for a song. Hailing from Europe, they have ensconced themselves in North American avifauna, breeding prolifically in urban concrete and suburban yards, producing five, six clutches of eggs a year, and aggressively outcompeting native birds for nest sites. Like European Americans, they are one of that continent's success stories in colonizing the New World.

Bluebird enthusiasts have done meticulous research on box design, with an aim to encouraging bluebird residency and making it difficult for house sparrows to use them. But the sparrows are persistent and flexible, and the battle is easily lost, as we discovered one spring a few years back. We were given several bluebird boxes that had originally been destined for use in a state park, and my husband put them up immediately, since it was already May. Within an hour after completing the task, we were astonished and delighted to observe a bluebird pair investigating one of the boxes. The birds perched on the roof and the female peered inside, as if to gauge the suitability of the family room. The male flapped busily about. The female flew to the maple tree, perhaps to think it over. It must have made a favorable impression, because after a day or two, the box was clearly theirs, and they began to set up housekeeping.

Within days, a second box was claimed by a pair of house sparrows. We were conversant with sparrow habits—how they will nest and renest, no matter how often one removes a nest—so we decided we would wait until there were eggs and then destroy the nest. We hoped, in a passive-aggressive way, to wear out the female. She could keep laying eggs—all that energy expended!—and we would keep destroying them, until she was sapped of her egg-laying ability. It seemed like a good plan.

Unfortunately, we never removed the eggs. The boxes were constructed so that the front panel could only be removed with a Phillips screwdriver. A Phillips screw is of no consequence to the structure of the box, but because this box had been destined for the park, the screw had been used to thwart park visitors who might open the box and disturb eggs or nestlings. Sadly, the screws also served to thwart us from taking action against the house sparrows. Our Phillips screwdriver is tucked away in the toolbox in the basement. Whenever we considered the undesirable birds in the nest box, we seemed to be either on our way out the door and into the car, or on our way out of the car and into the house to start supper, pick up the mess, feed the dog, or put away groceries.

The eggs became nestlings. Finally, one day, spurred by a conversation with a fellow Audubon member ("You have house sparrows in your nest box, I see," he noted in a meaningful tone of voice), I marched to the box, screwdriver in hand, and opened it. Huddled together in a fluff of gray downy feathers were eight charming baby birds, looking somewhat cross, rumpled, and vulnerable, as only baby birds can.

"Oh, the cute little birds!" our daughter cooed, as my husband held her up to see the nest. "See their big yellow beaks!" I could not bring myself to kill those birds and neither could my husband. The most we could do was flex our passive-aggressive muscles and let the front of the box hang open and hope that the babies would fall out of the nest prematurely—

or that a cat would conveniently come by. But of course, that didn't happen. The parents continued to feed them and care for them until they fledged. House sparrows are very adaptable.

Meanwhile, the bluebirds had been busy, too. After claiming their box, they built a tidy nest of fine grass, laid their eggs, and tended them carefully, day in and day out. They incubated the eggs during unseasonably hot weather, and I often observed the mother bird sitting faithfully on the nest, her small head close to the box opening, beak parted, panting. We worried about heat stroke.

We could tell when the eggs hatched. Both parents flew back and forth constantly, from nest box to garden, bringing grubs and insects to the ravenous nestlings. Once the little ones were fed, the parents departed with white fecal sacs in their beak, keeping the nest clean and free of excrement. This was the stage the bluebird nestlings were at when I opened the box on the house sparrows. The sparrows soon fledged, and we let the box open, removed the nest, and considered its use over for the year. We should not have been surprised when the resourceful sparrows transferred their interest to a new box, one located only feet from the occupied bluebird box. Within a day after our spotting the male house sparrow on the roof of the new box, its interior was filled with sticks and grass, the messy nest of the house sparrow. I had learned my lesson: don't even let the sparrows get started. I swept the box clean and kept it open. No more house sparrows in my yard.

If only I had a bird brain. The persistent house sparrows were not deterred. They merely turned their attention to their neighbor's box, landing on the bluebird's roof, peering inside, causing panic in the bluebird family. The frantic parents swooped at the intruders, chasing them away again and

again, only to have the would-be usurpers return, ever persistent. I became alarmed. House sparrows are known to
invade bluebird nests, kill off the nestlings by scalping them,
and build a nest on top of the bluebirds. It seemed likely that
this would happen in our yard. Over dinner, the sparrow-
bluebird drama unfolding outside the window, we pondered
our options. We decided to make the adjacent box available
and hope that the sparrows would return to their original
box, which we would then rigorously tend, destroying the
nests daily. The sparrows, doomed to continuous nest building, would be like Sisyphus, never completing the task at
hand.

We awoke the next morning to heavy rain. No birds were
in sight. Later, we spied the bluebirds huddled in the maple
tree. Rain ran off the female's beak; the male's head was
soaked. They made no visits to the nest box, and we were
sure the babies were dead. Several hours later, as the rain
let up, I glanced out the window to see the male sparrow
perched on the roof of his original box. Then, as I reached
for the binoculars, there was a flash of blue and the male
bluebird left his box, carrying a fecal sac. Both species in their
proper places. All was right with the world.

I have within me this irrational impulse not to intervene in
the ways of nature. I don't like to kill animals—each week I
deliberately avoid the spiders surviving in the corner of the
breakfast nook as I wash the kitchen floor. I don't even like
to thin carrots. Our badly degraded woods, which could be
managed so we could view the lake, are left to grow ever
more tangled, because I hear American redstarts singing
there, and I think they would nest more successfully in a
thick forest understory. At the same time, I eat meat, and I

will weed the carrots, consciously deciding to kill off lamb's quarters, pig sorrel, and quack grass. I know rationally that we are long past the time when we can adopt a hands-off approach and assume that nature will always right itself. We actually have positive proof of this: in a small portion of our woods, we have systematically removed the invasive shrub, buckthorn, and have been delighted to see a return of the desirable native shrub, wild cherry, in its place. When we deliberately took action to get rid of an intruder, the native species came back on its own.

Is it any different between house sparrows and eastern bluebirds? When I decided to let those sparrow nestlings live, in effect I was allowing eight additional house sparrows into the ecosystem. The bluebirds' chances of survival were that much more reduced by the addition of eight new competitors. "Not to decide is to decide" is the existential epigram. I did take action by not destroying that first sparrow nest. I was deciding against the bluebirds.

I could have instead adopted the approach my sister took when faced with a similar situation. In her case, the bluebird box was placed in the midst of her rock garden, and one May she had witnessed a bluebird pair repeatedly prevented from using the box by an aggressive set of sparrows. She had been diligent in cleaning out sparrow nests, but they hadn't shown any sign of discouragement. Finally, one day as she stood watering transplants, she witnessed another encounter between the species. Opening up the box, she discovered sparrow nestlings, and enraged momentarily beyond thought, she grabbed them one by one and drowned them in her bucket of water. As the last baby bird ceased to struggle in her hand, she regained her senses and was horrified at the sodden mass of feathers lying at her feet. But in that blind moment of passion, she had done what I had been unable to do, hindered by my misplaced sympathies: she had decided for the bluebirds.

My daughter had spoken with elemental attraction when she had cooed over the baby sparrows. The German ethologist Irenäus Eibl-Eibesfeldt undertook a study in the 1970s to determine why people were attracted to babies. He found that certain features—a rounded forehead, a human baby profile—elicited a "cute" response in his human test subjects. The baby birds were perfect models to call forth a "cute" response in me, and it worked: I let them live.

It is a strange mix of emotion and reason we carry inside our heads—a passion for babies, a passion for feathered nestlings; a love of the wild, the native, the beautiful; a disdain for the drab, the commonplace, the invader. I think I know what is best from an ecological point of view, informed by my training, my studies, and the research, and then emotion sweeps in to either enable me to act rightly or to hinder me from acting at all. Who can say with certainty what the turbulent inner workings will produce in any one situation?

Five days after watching the house sparrows and bluebirds sort it out, each to its own nest box, I realized that the bluebirds were not attending the nest box anymore. Instead, they seemed to be everywhere in the yard: on the clothesline, the garden trellis, the maple tree, with the male singing his bubbling territorial song. Damn! Had my attentiveness driven them away after all? Other birds now came to their vacated box—tree swallows, house sparrows, even a wren, thinking big.

"What's with the bluebirds, Mom?" my son asked.

"I don't know," I told him. "I'm too afraid to look." I imagined a fluff of small, life-less feathers, the eyes involuted and empty. Together, we stiffened our spines, took up the Phillips screwdriver, and went out to open the box. We undid the door and peered inside. The nest was completely empty. All that remained was the tidy construction of soft, woven grass. "They're gone!" we exclaimed together, feeling as if we were looking at the empty tomb, witnesses of the resurrection. "They did it! They made it!" And now somewhere, two young fledglings and two busy parents were in the wide world, on their own, beyond the ministrations of our well-meaning care.

I brushed out the nest, shut up the door, and screwed in the screw. All was now ready for the second clutch of eggs.

# Conspiracy

Last week was the festival of Pentecost, an event taking place fifty days after Easter. According to the story, the apostles were gathered in one place when there was a rush of wind and small flickers of flame rested over their heads. Marked by fire, they went out and discovered they had the ability to communicate in many languages. It's a strange tale and one the Lutherans have been squeamish acknowledging, not wanting to be lumped with the charismatic Christians and their odd and disconcerting penchant to speak in tongues, a babble of nonsense syllables. But celebrate, we did. The liturgical color for Pentecost is red, the color of the Church, and the sanctuary was hung with lengths of scarlet ribbon that undulated like tongues with every wisp of a breeze. In the Bible, the presence of the Spirit is denoted by a dove, by the wind, or by fire. These natural phenomena, bird, wind, and fire, make the Spirit seem less strange and supernatural and more ever present, more of a common occurrence in the world.

The pastor talked about the "conspiracy of Christianity"—*con* meaning "with" and *spire* meaning "to breathe," or all of us breathing together. But in truth, all of life is part of a conspiracy. All, save for a very few bacterial and algal forms, take in oxygen from the atmosphere, which becomes part of the body. All later release those molecules back, where they can be taken up by someone else, so that we all have the essence of elephant and earwig, dinosaur and dinoflagellate in us, breathing together, the great conspiracy of life. As if in agreement with this scientific observation, the Gospel writer Luke, who tells the Pentecost story, records Peter's proclamation that God will "pour out his Spirit upon all flesh," a nice inclusive note.

I have been thinking about the spirit that resides in living things recently, after a conversation with environmentalist friends. We had been discussing a rough draft of an essay, and two of them, both men, had made strong, impassioned cases for hunting, fishing, and trapping as essential, instinctive activities connecting humans with nature. This is not a new idea. I would wager that most of the men I know who hunt or fish would agree, and in fact, sportsmen and their organizations are often among the most impassioned conservationists. Ducks Unlimited and Pheasants Forever restore habitat, preserve wetlands and grasslands, and hold great educational programs. Men who tromp around in a fall cornfield or sit huddled in a blind in a damp marsh talk about an almost mystical communion with the ancient rhythms of life. There is a deep, primal satisfaction in knowing one's place in the food chain, in the web of life. When one sits down to a meal of wild game or fresh fish from a Minnesota lake, there is unity with nature that most domesticated, technological humans have largely forgotten.

I haven't owned a fishing license in ten years, since my children got old enough to bait their own hooks and take their fish off the line. But I grew up fishing—I know the utter thrill of hauling in an impossibly long northern pike. I have felt wonder in beholding the beauty of a pumpkin seed sunfish, with its buttery yellow belly, emerging from an ordinary lake. I love it when my sons bring home their catch for me to fry— so long as they clean it—and I sit down to a meal with gusto.

But I no longer fish, for a number of reasons. For one, I haven't seen a sunfish bigger than my hand in decades. Each summer weekend, I see the boat landings on the Chisago Lakes packed with dozens of boat trailers in their parking lots. I note ten or twelve boats clustered around a fishing hole, every boat undoubtedly equipped with sonar, and I have no desire to add to the pressure on our fish populations. But perhaps more significantly, I have become squeamish about killing. One swift knock to the head, one decisive slice of the fillet knife. The fish suffers very little. But I am stunned by how swiftly the spirit drains—the beauty fades, the vitality ceases, the iridescence dulls. The animal leaves the conspiracy, and I do not want to be the agent of that.

My environmental friends didn't focus on fishing, however. The essay under discussion pondered trapping, and one of the men, who had trapped when younger, reminisced about the odd but pleasant fragrance of a dried muskrat skin, of the satisfying enactment of the ancient art of setting traps, and of skinning the catch and making a pelt. This man told of a particularly skilled trapper who was quick and agile in skinning, who approached trapped animals with such guile that they showed no fear. He killed them quickly, with little suffering (save, of course, for the leg in the jaws of the trap). I tried to go there. I imagined the native trappers, treading over snowdrifts on handmade snowshoes. I thought about my far-distant ancestors, living in northern Europe and keeping warm with animal skins. It is very probable that were it not for their skill in trapping, I would not be here in my warm house heated by fossil fuels. I considered the human place in nature, in the broad scheme of things.

Then I thought about foxes.

We have red foxes in the vicinity of Pioneer Lake. I see them very infrequently—a flash of fur crossing ahead of me on the road when I'm out on a run, a streak disappearing into the weeds in the glare of a headlight. One Valentine's Day, I looked out the window at sunset to see two foxes zip past, one in hot pursuit of the other. I thought at first they were two large, orange cats, until I realized how unlikely that would be, when our neighborhood doesn't even have one orange cat. It was no gross misjudgment—red fox are not very big, about ten to fourteen pounds, about the weight of our gray tabby.

One fall afternoon awhile back, my husband and I were hiking in cutover woods north of the Minnesota border when we were joined by a fox that followed us for half an hour. Evidently just curious, it paused when we stopped to turn and study it, then resumed dogging us from a distance of twenty feet when we continued down the path. We had a very close view of its beautiful auburn fur, its dainty black stockings, the endearing tilt to its ears, and its yellow cat-like eyes.

Then I imagined one of those foxes caught in a trap. The surprise, the pain, the terror as the jaw snaps with a click. The trapper approaches and speaks to the animal in a sing-song voice, mesmerizing it so that its curiosity gets the better of its fear. To the fox, the trapper becomes an oddity. To the trapper, the fox is—what? Beauty? Grace? Prey? Money? Probably all of these, and I will not diminish the trapper's spiritual sense that somehow the two are bound in an ancient relationship.

Then what happens? A swift rap on the muzzle renders the fox unconscious; a twist of the vertebral column takes its breath away. "Man always kills the thing he loves," writes ecologist Aldo Leopold, but must we do this? Are we so caught in the ancient relationship that to deny it, or defy it, as some animal rights activists do, is to deny our full connection to nature?

Perhaps this is a male/female thing. The one other woman joining us in the discussion did not leap to the argument that hunting is "hard-wired" into humans and was quick to point out how the hard-wired argument has been misused to justify all manner of abuse against women. But let's play with the trapping/hunting-is-innate idea for a bit. Like most biologists, I fall back on biology as explanation for all sorts of behavior that seem hard to alter. We tend to view those who reject a biological basis as naive at best. The majority of hunters and trappers are men; even most anglers are men. As the evolutionary argument goes, in our ancient past, men were the hunters and women the gatherers. Consequently, the urge to track and kill an animal was more essential for a male than a female, and there must have been a high selective value on the activity—those who were good at it were warmer and well fed and produced more children than their less-skilled neighbors. The propensity to learn those skills was biologically based, and the children inherited it.

This is dicey reasoning, however. It is only conjecture and doesn't explain those men who have no interest in and, in fact, decry the activity. Moreover, a biological basis doesn't automatically transfer over to a moral imperative. At best, it is useful only to hint at what we're dealing with. If, indeed, evolution has bestowed on men an instinct to hunt and trap, then that inclination would be difficult to eradicate. And it would explain why I am simply unable to follow my male friends' passion for the activity.

Imagine the North American continent before the European settlement. Forests so continuous that a squirrel could travel from the Atlantic shore to the Mississippi and never set paw on the ground; mass movement of passenger pigeons so dense that it darkened the sky *for days*. And I don't have to rely on these old saws to tell me about the once-abundant life in North America. I can open my grandparents' photo album and see the unbelievable number of northern pike taken from Lake Vermillion in one day, my grandfather in his teens, skinny and smiling beside the heavily laden stringer.

Part of the reason I recoil from trapping and hunting is the same reason that I no longer fish: wildlife is no longer abundant, and pressure on it is intensifying. One time while out running, I heard a pheasant crow and then witnessed five hunters scour the cornfield for that one bird. Though our game populations, as well as the furbearing animals, are "managed" by the Department of Natural Resources, almost never are the populations at pre-European settlement levels. A few species are—white-tailed deer and Canada geese— and my stomach doesn't knot when I hear of hunters bringing home this game.

The main reason that wildlife populations are not as large as in pre-European settlement days is that we have eradicated habitat and replaced it with agricultural fields, pastures, and residential areas. And we can clothe ourselves with what we produce using the land in this way: cotton, wool, cow leather, and synthetics from the fossil fuels we are consuming in large quantity, at great cost to the ecosystem. The need to use wild animals for clothing is long gone. By trapping them, we deliver a double whammy: we've greatly reduced their habitat, and we still act as predator.

But numbers aren't my only stumbling block. As I have grown older, I have become more interested in the particular, in individuals rather than in populations. Every animal shot by a .22 or caught in a leg trap has a past. If a mammal, it was nursed by a mother and cared for in a tender, animal way. If a bird, its mother risked her life to keep eggs warm in storms and frigid weather. It survived the perils of immaturity,

spent its days honing its skill in acquiring food, sought out
the company of its own kind, or traveled in the presence of
its siblings, which it knew well in an animal way. Each individual is a tiny window into a different, nonhuman world,
a glimpse into an alternative way of living on this planet,
and I am thrilled when I can watch and try to get inside its
head for a time.

So it seems somehow wrong, for me at least, that we tinker with the conspiracy—those who breathe together—when
we don't have to, when we're not dependent on wild animals to feed or clothe us. As them, I just want to live. I don't
want to take anyone's breath away.

# Illumined Courtship

The heat is on. Humidity saturates the air, making it work to breathe. At night, I seek any waft of a breeze, my skin finely tuned to cooling drafts. Thunderstorms punctuate these high summer days, releasing torrents of rain with a tropical flourish.

I awoke to an approaching storm last week. Lightning flashed on the far western horizon, illuminating the sky at 2:00 A.M. Rising from bed, I stumbled out to the living room to gauge the storm's approach. How soon would it be here? Was it time to close windows? The night was particularly dark. Clouds had already moved in, erasing the stars. But as if to compensate for the loss of their heavenly sparkle, the meadow fronting our yard was a-twinkle with moving pinpoints of light. They glowed with a brilliant greenish hue, winking on and off as if imparting a code.

Fireflies!

What is more mesmerizing than a firefly? Some phenomena of nature seem so improbable that it is hard to believe they exist. The pure red of a vermilion flycatcher, the long migration of the seemingly fragile monarch butterfly, the drawn-out tinkling song of the winter wren—how are these things possible? Fireflies fall into that category: insects that emit bright flashes of light.

It astonishes me to recall that I was almost grown when I first encountered fireflies. Growing up in a newly formed

1950s suburb, I read about the summer lights of lightning bugs in books, children's novels that were almost always set in New England or upstate New York, hardly ever in the Midwest. I assumed they were an East Coast marvel, too exotic for the prosaic plains states. Laura Ingalls Wilder never mentioned fireflies.

Now I realize that what my childhood lacked wasn't pizzazz, but simply habitat. Up and down the asphalt streets, block after block, the neatly tended lawns were mowed to a fine carpet. The tousled straggle of old-field growth in vacant lots that might have harbored fireflies had been beaten into submission. Our neighborhood had once been a cow pasture. No native meadow plants remained.

What a pity. Having one's imagination sparked by nature is the birthright of every child. And sadly, most children who lack fireflies on summer evenings don't realize that a hole is present in the dusk, don't miss them, and so will never know that the world is infused with this kind of magic. "Fairies!" I thought, when I first saw them as a teenager. I had read *Peter Pan*. At last, I understood Tinkerbell.

Fireflies aren't only about fairies and magic, of course. They have other critical tales to tell. Minnesota has fifteen species of fireflies, according to specimens in museums, and I have seen at least two in recent days in the meadows alongside Pioneer Lake. I haven't taken a net and gone after them, but different species have different flash patterns and different times of activity. I've encountered one species at twilight, twinkling from the vegetation as the western sky remains rosy from the setting sun. It was a different species cruising about in the middle of the night, when I observed the approaching storm.

In each case, when they flash their little lanterns, located on the undersides of their abdomens, the fireflies are searching for mates. Typically, males fly three or four feet above the meadows' upper reaches, flashing a characteristic pattern of set duration and number of flashes. At dusk, females sit atop the pinnacle of a slender stalk of grass or goldenrod, or a bush, awaiting the right male. When a female sees a flash pattern that interests her, she answers back with a flash of her own. Different species have different flash patterns, so each firefly mates with its own kind.

After an exchange of light messages, males locate females on their perches, where mating occurs. Later, females lay their eggs on the ground or in the soil, where they hatch into larvae. The grub-like larvae live at or below the soil surface where they remain all winter. That is the textbook account of firefly courtship, but everyone knows that romance is much more messy. The atmosphere of illumined courtships, however graceful at first glance, apparently resembles more of the rumbles from *West Side Story* ("Hey, Baby, let's go for a riiiide!") and less of the charm of *A Midsummer's Night Dream* (two sets of lovers in a magical forest).

In my meadow I can see the high-flying males and the sedate, positioned females. What I don't see, what is not obvious, are the undercurrents of rivalry, deceit, and treachery swirling around the luminescent insects. As is so often the case, competition for females is intense among males. A coy female may flash in response to a cruising male—and researchers think females go for the biggest, brightest flashers—of course! But once she responds, there are often many males nearby, ready, willing, and able to mate with her. What results is a mad scramble, on foot, to the perched female. Here's how an article in the eminent *Journal of Insect Behavior* describes a tryst: "Once on foot, rival males scurry toward the female and often physically jostle for access to her, forming 'love-knots' of suitors."

The twinkling meadow is also rife with another type of intrigue, and those who believe nature reveals the hand of God would do well to ponder this. In the meadow, perched on grass stalks as well, may be a second species of firefly, with something other than romance on her little insect mind. Researchers have known for years that females of the genus *Photuris* will answer the flash of males of the genus *Photinus* and lure them to their perches—but not to mate with them. Such cross-species mating would not produce offspring, by definition. Their aim is rather to eat the *Photinus* males, a seemingly bizarre behavior, since adult fireflies of both species are not known to eat much of anything.

The deceiving females share one thing: they have already been mated and seldom respond to their own males' flash patterns any longer. They are interested in the patterns of other species, however, and actively attract, capture, and devour them. These females have been called femme fatales by the (male) researcher who first unraveled their web of deception. It seems like a heavy moniker to hang on a little beetle, but the dictionary definition fits: a woman whose seductive charms may lead a man into compromising or dangerous situations.

The heat is on. On sultry days like this one, I am reminded of the steamy classic film *A Streetcar Named Desire* with the young Marlon Brando bellowing "Stella!" and the sweltering sense of summery New Orleans that even the fake sets of the French Quarter convey. It amuses me to imagine our meadow as a similar stage on which couples are bound by irresistible attraction.

Most animals are secretive when they mate. While intent on procreating, they are vulnerable to ever present predators.

By necessity, for preservation purposes, the act must be short, sweet, and secluded.

But imagine Stanley using a flashlight to come on to Stella. Immediately, the clandestine becomes conspicuous, at least to visually oriented observers. When fireflies flash, a whole host of others are alerted, including birds, the most likely predator of small beetles. Human researchers, themselves visually attuned, love this—they can actually see males and females communicate (contrast this with a species that relies primarily on pheromones—humans are totally out of the loop). Humans can even participate in the exchange, using a flashlight.

Fireflies have evolved a means of protecting themselves against predators. Apparently, they don't taste good. Mice, and some species of birds and bats, are known to avoid them. While they flash to their potential mates, they are also communicating with potential predators: if you eat me, you'll be sorry.

The heat is on. At sunset on hot July days, we breathe a sigh of relief for the respite of the night. In the darkening evening, I look out over the meadow and consider the steamy insect sex going on there.

# The Bullhead Queen

Buried somewhere in the weeds at the far edges of our yard lies the Bullhead Queen. A remnant of our family's past, it has been neglected so long that I cannot even find it in the lush growth of summer. Rather, I wait for it to reappear each fall when the tall grasses, struck by frost, die back and reveal the Queen, faded and aging fast. Despite her grand name, the Queen was little more than a wooden raft, something Huck Finn might have recognized. I'm not certain she was even seaworthy or if her builders ever took her out for a spin on the lake. I'm quite sure I would be the last to know.

The Bullhead Queen was nailed together by my oldest son and one of his friends, our next-door neighbor. They worked diligently one summer, salvaging wood from discarded construction lumber, measuring, sawing, pounding, painting. They even fashioned a chair of sorts, so that the person propelling the craft would ride high out of the water. On the back of this chair is the Queen's finest feature, a credible depiction of a bullhead, rendered in leftover oils from a paint-by-number kit, complete with beady eyes and whiskery barbels.

The Queen's shipwrights were fourteen that summer, old enough and vigorous enough to be consumed by masculine restlessness, but too young to work at paying jobs or drive cars. The ironically named Queen represented an escape from the female-dominated world of their mothers and sisters, and promised autonomy on the high seas of Pioneer Lake, bordering our backyard. As the summer wore on and it became evident that the Queen would not be completed before the start of school, their ardor did not flag. The dream of independence was enough to sustain their effort.

The Queen was aptly named, as bullheads are the dominant fish in Pioneer. As a consequence, they reigned as the chief piscine interest of the boys. Both families had only recently moved to Pioneer's shores, and together the boys honed their fishing skills. During the first summer, they focused on the simple mechanics of fishing. The lake and the bullheads were wonderful teachers. They learned to be creative with bait—corn, marshmallows, bits of hot dog could draw a bite. They learned to be wary of wicked spines when extracting a wriggling fish from a hook. They learned how to clean a fish and, after that, discovered that bullheads were perhaps not the best for eating.

Then summer drew to a close and the tackle boxes, rods, and reels were stashed in the corner of the garage. But the education continued. In the halls of the middle school, a common topic among the boys in the Chisago Lakes area was the art of angling. Some had fish houses on the lakes in winter. Some hauled sleds out and tended open holes. Everyone shared information on what was biting and on what type of lure was preferred. In the spring, the boys came home from school talking about crappie holes, panfish, and five-pound northerns caught in shallow water by people standing on docks. The boys became immersed in a whole culture of fishing.

One of the sacred texts of the sect of the angler is a monthly magazine, *In-Fisherman: The Journal of Freshwater Fishing*. *In-Fisherman* is distributed nationally, but it comes out of Brainerd, arguably the fishing capital of Minnesota. Each issue sports well-written articles on all aspects of fishing. There are regular columns, even one dedicated to philosophizing about this addictive activity. The fourteen-year-olds read the magazine religiously. The boys, who had previously gone on jags involving dinosaurs, birds of prey, and natural disasters, now turned their focus on finny denizens of the deep.

One perennial topic in *In-Fisherman* that especially intrigued them was the Bass Tournament. From reading the magazine, they learned that fishing could appeal to their competitive natures, as well as satisfy that primal urge to hunt. The money, the glamour, and the lure of competition made a bass tournament so attractive. But the future in which they actually might enter a bass tournament was a long way off.

Fourteen is a pivotal age for boys. Moody, energetic, but often aimless, they are cutting their teeth on new thoughts, trying on adult intellect. It's the age of irreverence, a time for a first flirtation with satire. It is the year of *Mad Magazine*. *Mad Magazine* coupled with *In-Fisherman* in the fertile imagination of a young teen produces unexpected results. One day I came upon the boys working on a computer drawing of a bewhiskered fish that could be transferred to a T-shirt. Surrounding the fish was the caption "Pioneer Lake, Quality Bullheads since 1998." It was to be the official garb of participants in the first annual Bullhead Tournament.

The black-and-white photo shows four boys crouched, smiling, in front of a sagging six-person tent. It's a summer day. The boys are dressed in shorts and oversized T-shirts. Three have baseball caps shielding their faces; the fourth, handsome even in gawky adolescence, wears a shirt with a computer-generated bullhead on it.

These boys will remain friends throughout high school. Before a Bible camp canoe trip, they will argue to take their rods and reels along, pointing out that several key disciples were fishermen. In their senior year, the Pioneer Lake boys will drive to school with a canoe strapped to the top of the car so that during a study hall, when they are allowed off campus, they can fish in nearby South Center Lake. At graduation, they will choose to walk in together to the strains of "Pomp and Circumstance." They will follow wildly different paths when they leave home. One will develop a passion for geology; one will endure the rigorous engineering program of the Coast Guard Academy; one will become an elite high jumper in college, dividing his time between fishing and the track and field team; and one will join the Marines and invade Iraq.

Yet fishing will continue to unite them. Their friendship will strain under the pull of different views of the world, different experiences, different timetables. The bond of the Brotherhood of Anglers, though, will prove as tensile as a hundred-pound test line.

At the moment the shutter clicks and their image burns into the film, they know none of this. They are fourteen. It is summer vacation and they are posing by their catch. Quite secondary to the fishermen, a mess of bullheads has been dumped on the lawn and appears in the foreground of the photo. The fish are small, no more than six inches in length, and numerous, maybe two dozen in all. Even though every boy in the photo has at one time or another hauled in a truly wonderful walleye or notable northern pike, they are all looking pleased at what the Bullhead Tournament has produced.

There was more to the tournament than the bullheads, of course. There was the night in the tent, the identical T-shirts, the twenty-four pack of Mountain Dew, the day on the water, the jokes, and the stories, true and not true. And of course, the Queen, already relegated to the weeds.

Years later, I will ask my son, "And then what? Did you weigh them?" (thinking of plastic bags and my bathroom scale). No. "Did you have prizes for the biggest or the most caught?" No. "Did you fish at night?" No.

"We were just having fun, Mom."

Grown now, the Bullhead Tournament participants do serious fishing these days. They head to Bemidji or the Boundary Waters; they seek out a certain bay in nearby Chisago Lake that is usually good for bass at sunset. They fish off the stress of high-level engineering classes, the pressure to perform on research projects. They fish off the terror of combat, the frustration of ill-conceived romances, the uncertainty of the future that is part of every young adulthood.

One thing they do not do is compete in bass tournaments. They know that fishing is not about catching the biggest fish. It is not really about catching any fish at all. It doesn't matter a whit if they only catch bullheads, though usually they're after northerns or walleye these days.

When all is said and done, it doesn't really matter that the Bullhead Queen couldn't float. She was a splendid craft to launch fourteen-year-olds into manhood.

# Skiing at Flamin' Feet

When the little plastic buoys appeared on our lake a few years ago, I was both startled and curious. Pioneer Lake had sported just one buoy the past summer. I assumed it marked a spot where lake clarity was being monitored. The Minnesota Pollution Control Agency (MPCA) organizes volunteers to observe lakes through the open water season. I'd been surprised that humble Pioneer had a monitor, but when the MPCA released the compiled data on Minnesota lakes, Pioneer's records were in the ranks. They showed what anyone could see with the naked eye: clarity in Pioneer was never any greater than two feet and usually less.

The buoy pattern was reminiscent of a hopscotch board, the kind children draw on schoolyard sidewalks. It wasn't long before I found out what they were. They marked a slalom ski course. It amazed me that a private party could commandeer a public waterway for personal use. I was further astonished when I found out that it could be done without public input and that a ski course is in the same official category as a swimming raft anchored off shore. Its regulation came under the jurisdiction of the Chisago County Sheriff, not the Minnesota Department of Natural Resources (DNR), and such a course could be sited anywhere, without regard to shoreline erosion or wildlife disturbance. All that is needed is a permit (which is free), an insurance binder, and the assurance that the course is placed out of the way of major boat traffic. Nobody monitors whether running such a course adversely affects resident wildlife, or whether the wake kicked up by frequent passes in a motorboat affects the stability of the adjacent shoreline.

Some neighbors on the lake were unhappy, and their murmurings soon reached our ears. The course was situated closer to the western shore, and we on the east side heard that western shoreline owners were concerned. They thought the steep clay banks of their property were being eaten away by the lap of waves from the skiers' boats. (I must note that these are banks where the native vegetation has been removed, possibly for a view.) We easterners had more modest banks and no noticeable erosion.

One day a nice-looking young man came knocking on our door. In his hand was a petition seeking support for the ski course. A few neighbors had already signed on. I asked him about the course. How long would it be up? How often would it be used? He said he would train from May through October (he would obviously employ a wet suit during some months). Would I sign the petition?

"Well, I don't know," I hedged, not wanting to antagonize him. "Migrating ducks use the lake in the fall. How do I know they won't be disturbed by a noisy boat going back and forth?"

"Oh, I never see any birds when I'm out on the lake," he reassured me.

"Yes, but I'm the president of Wild River Audubon," I replied, testily. "It's not simply a matter of me signing on. I need to see data that the birds aren't affected!" At this point the encounter assumed a surly nature and the petitioner went away.

Within a week, we received an invitation to attend an organizational meeting for the Pioneer Lake Association. Many lakes in Minnesota, especially big, popular recreational lakes, have such groups formed by lakeshore owners. Associations serve to protect their lakes from the types of use that degrade them. Lake associations address important concerns like the spread of Eurasian water milfoil and zebra mussels, the loss of buffer strips to cleanse runoff entering the lake, and the use of pesticides and fertilizers in the lake's watershed. They are great venues for exchanging information and for neighbors to work together to protect their chief asset. It was perhaps a bit odd for modest little Pioneer to have a lake association, but heck, it had a clarity monitor, so why not? I thought the proposal was a good idea.

The first (and ultimately, final) organizational meeting was scheduled on an evening I couldn't attend, and consequently the details of the ruckus that ensued are only hearsay. Apparently, it was a scrappy, barely civilized brawl over the ski course, bank erosion, and the use of a lake of modest dimensions. Somehow, a "constitution" of the incipient association emerged out of the uproar and circulated among the neighbors, to be signed for approval. Among its provisions was a rule that members must approach the association with any concerns before contacting the DNR. Somehow that didn't seem right to me, and I didn't sign it—nor to my knowledge did anyone else.

Mulling it over, I decided that the proposed creation of an association was Phase Two of the attempt by the skiers to enlist, or coerce, the support of the neighbors. But for neighbors who liked to live in harmony, the mere whisper that a lake association might be in actuality a battleground was enough to nix it. Thus, the opportunity for fruitful conversation on the use of a small lake died.

But the ski course did not. It bloomed again the following May, its nineteen buoys reemerging, a now-permanent artificial fixture in the natural landscape. A regulation water-ski course is 850 feet long, and boats and skiers need a minimum of a 600-foot approach on either end, so the entire space used is at least 2,000 feet in length, just under half a mile. The width is narrower, only 75 feet with 100-foot safety margins on either side. To be a good training area, a course needs to be in a sheltered portion of a lake or river, free of backwash from other boats and out of the way of heavy boat traffic.

Pioneer fits these specifications well. Because of its modest size with no public access and no game fish, and surely because of its water color, a rich pea green, there had been no motorboats on its waters before the course came into being. Water quality had been a determination for recreational pursuits since the outlet to North Center had been blocked and the one-time marsh became a lake. We owned a little paddleboat and a canoe, as did several of our neighbors, and on occasion we'd paddle out on a summer evening, exploring the shores.

With the advent of a small, suburban-type development on the northwest shore came a suburban-type interest in motorized water activity. The much larger lakes in the area had become built-up years ago. The few remaining lots on these lakes now sell for nearly a million dollars. It seemed that motorized recreational users now viewed Pioneer favorably, despite its hue. The skiers all live in this new neighborhood.

What is the attraction of a slalom ski course? The sport is precise and demanding. It is a high-skill activity that requires strength and agility from the skier, maneuvering around the buoys while being timed. It takes the activity of waterskiing to the next level, when skiers become "bored by just kicking up a lot of spray on a single ski," as one Web site put it. From asking around, I learned that several skiers use Pioneer's slalom ski course (none would talk to me). One, in fact, a fourteen-year-old boy, is a champion. A submitted article to the local paper lauded his "tremendously successful competitive barefoot waterskiing season," in which he earned two silver and two gold medals. The article added that he trained at the Flamin' Feet Barefoot Water Ski Training Center in Center City. I had no idea that Pioneer Lake had such status!

What I do know is that the course is used constantly. Throughout the summer months, the skiers are out there every night from late afternoon until shortly after sunset, when dusk draws a curtain on activity. On weekends, there is a continuous roar of motors. In this, Pioneer is no different from many Minnesota lakes—only a lot smaller.

Pop! Pop! The sound of a shotgun bursts open the predawn quiet of Saturday morning. In bed in the gray light, I check the clock—6:25. I assume it is precisely thirty minutes before sunrise. This is when hunting can commence. Geese are clamoring, sputtering, frantically trying to maneuver into a spot of safety. I can hear their wings beat the water. The racket continues for about twenty minutes. That is how long it takes for all the Canada geese and the sprinkling of ducks on the water—those that didn't immediately succumb to a shell—to reposition themselves at the far end of the lake. That end is firmly within Center City limits, where the discharge of firearms is prohibited.

While out rowing on the lake, I had come across the hunter's crudely constructed blind, a drape of dark material concealing a hollowed out portion of the alder thicket.

The hunter sits behind the blind on a folding chair. I know the hunter, like the skiers, only by the accoutrements of his activity on the lake. My guess is that he has hunted on Pioneer for decades, since before it became populated with suburban houses ringing its shore. It is bizarre having a duck hunter sitting in a blind five hundred yards from where we sit at our breakfast table eating pancakes. "I can't imagine what kind of hunting experience he gets out of Pioneer," a hunter friend remarked to me.

When I first learned that the slalom course would be utilized through October, I was intrigued. The course is a mere fifty yards or less from the hunting blind. How would that play out? But the users subdivide the resource very well. The hunter is in his blind only until eight o'clock or so. The skiers don't appear until at least ten.

"I don't know why you're so bent out of shape about that ski course, Mom," my oldest son tells me. "After all, they're at least using the lake." I'm not sure I'm bent out of shape. I am rankled at times when I pass the southern shore and, gazing out over the placid water, see the surface marred by artificial buoys. I can't imagine imposing my activities on the greater populace in such a way. But I'll admit that I am impressed by the skiers' lack of squeamishness. Anyone immersing himself for hours at a time in Pioneer's thick, smelly algal soup is not timid.

My son's comment interests me, though. It rattles about in my thoughts long after the clatter of the skiers' outboard motor has died away for the evening. What do we mean by *use of the lake*? We often tell friends that we use the lake more in winter than in summer. By that we mean we're more often out on it when the lake is frozen and we glide across its surface on skates or skis.

Sometimes we take a canoe out when the water is open.

At twilight we paddle the shoreline, enjoying the blooming summer flowers—the dusty pink of joe-pye weed or the creamy white of turtle's head. We see if we can locate the wood duck family or edge closer to a great blue heron, frozen in the shallows, hunting for supper. It's difficult, though. They almost always spook before we get very near. As the leggy heron takes wing, I wonder where it and the other wading birds go when the skiers are out each evening. Do they cringe in the shadows or abandon Pioneer for less occupied space?

Asserting that at least the skiers are using the lake implies that this is the order of things. Lakes are meant to be used, as are the trees in the forest, fish in the ocean, gravel in glacial deposits, and geese resting on water. The assertion begs the question, what is the purpose of a lake? Why is it here?

These questions are quaint, if not absurd. Lakes have no obvious reason for being here, no purpose. They were formed by the retreat of the glaciers after the most recent ice age, that's all.

But we do use our lakes. Pioneer, balanced on that precarious divide between rural and urban development, is used by two types of people. One user is extractive, taking something from the water. The second is noisy and possessive, spilling over into commonly held space. The quiet types—the paddlers, quackers, honkers, waders—are left to fend for themselves, to fit themselves, if they can, into smaller and smaller niches.

When we settled on Pioneer Lake over a decade ago, it was a magnet for migrating waterfowl. Spring and fall, tremendous flocks of geese would rest on its waters, their continuous gabbling filling the air, day and night. Ducks arrived in spurts, with an air of randomness. Scaup one day, teal the next. Sometimes ringed-necks, sometimes redhead—all common birds. I took to scanning the water with my binocs in hopes of spotting something rare, perhaps a widgeon or a pintail.

Wildlife biologists agree that the 1990s saw a moderate increase in breeding ducks in our state. But recently, the trend has been downward, with fewer and fewer birds both migrating through and remaining to nest and raise families. Certain species, like pintails and canvasbacks, are becoming scarce. Fluctuations in the waterfowl population are not uncommon and are well studied by state biologists because there's money in ducks. In 2004, eighty-nine thousand Minnesotans held duck-hunting licenses, the highest in the nation.

Federal biologists have studied duck populations and habitat for fifty years, believed to be the largest long-term wildlife survey in the world. The reasons for the decline in ducks are many. Chief among them is the loss of habitat, the main reason most animals go extinct. Most waterfowl in Minnesota depend on an extensive habitat of "prairie potholes"— small marshes offering protection and food for breeding birds. People refer to these wetlands as "duck factories." Although they are now protected, these have been drained for agriculture and urban development since the onset of European settlement. In the 150 years since the Europeans arrived in large numbers in Minnesota, we have lost 90 percent of our prairie wetlands. That alone is sufficient to cause a decline in ducks.

But loss of habitat is not the whole story. Invasive species, like carp and hybrid cattail, upset the ecological balance that provides food for waterfowl. Hunting pressure could play a role. Wildlife specialists point out that ducks are wary birds, and with eighty-nine thousand Minnesotans waiting in blinds for them to land on the water, hunting pressure is intense.

Last, increased motorized activity on lakes means that the birds are disturbed not only during their breeding season but during spring and fall migrations. Migration is stressful for birds. A duck can lose 10 to 15 percent of its body weight in a single day of flying. It needs time to recover after a long day. In good habitat, it can gain back its weight in one to three days. If disturbed, it takes longer, from five to nine days.

Imagine being an exhausted duck, sinking to rest on the small, protected surface of Pioneer. If it is a Monday, you may be in luck. The lake is placid and quiet. But if it's a Saturday, there will be a hunter hidden in the alder thicket that seems to offer such good cover. A motorboat towing a human will spend several hours running the ski course, and the incessant noise alone will convince you that this particular patch of water is not the safe stopover it seems. But where to go? The larger lakes are far too busy, the smaller ponds have been ditched and drained. Geese are heading to nearby fields to glean corn or oats, but for a dabbling duck, a marsh is necessary.

In fine, multiple-use fashion, the people around Pioneer have many ways to outcompete the birds for use of this limited resource: hunting, noisemaking, running motor boats, and of course, grooming manicured suburban lawns, destroying their habitat. Really, the ducks we have should be considered small miracles.

On Monday morning, after people have left for work and school, I walk down to our dock to observe the geese muttering to themselves on the south end of the lake. Far off to the north, I see the silhouette of three ducks, resting on the water.

# The Green Season

When I look out over the meadow this August morning, the landscape is washed almost entirely in green. The variety of hues is dazzling. There's the lawn, which can only be described as "grass green," and the two maples with their three-pointed, hand-like leaves that are still in sprightly summer verdure. The many herbaceous plants of the meadow are beginning to add some golden tones to the palette, and what once was bright and true is more faded and mature, jaundiced, olive and ochre. All too soon the vibrant scene will be colored by the warm yellows of autumn, but this week we still bask in the green season.

Of all the sunlight emitted by the glowing orb that forms the center of our solar system, only a fraction of the spectrum is green. Just a small portion of the sun's light, in fact, actually reaches the earth's surface. The highest-energy light rays, gamma and X rays, and most ultraviolet rays hit the earth's atmosphere and bounce back into space. The longest rays penetrate the atmosphere—that insulating blanket that wraps the planet—and warm its surface. We call them "infrared," and a nonphysicist might be best acquainted with them in everyday life, when staying at a ritzy hotel, where such rays are often used as overhead heaters in bathrooms.

Of more significance, perhaps, in our lives is the narrow band of rays that animals on earth can see, the ones to which they have evolved sense organs. We call it "visible light," and it is only about 14 percent of all the solar radiation that comes through the atmosphere. I used to think it was amazing that our eyes were evolved to see light that reaches the earth rather than the wavelengths that don't. What a happy coincidence! But think about it: obviously, animals wouldn't evolve a sense organ to perceive something that isn't there.

The shortest wavelengths we perceive are violet, the longest are red. Somewhere in the middle, at a length of about 5,400 angstroms, is what is lighting up my room, green light. It is the hue to which the human eye is most sensitive.

The greenness of the summer world is most striking in the spring, when color returns after a winter spent in monochrome. One April, I spent a week in Louisiana, paddling the bayou outside of New Orleans. I had never experienced the terrain of the Mississippi delta, with its broad sweeping grasses and subtropical palms. My eyes were accustomed to Minnesota's grays and whites, and on my first morning there, Louisiana seemed unbelievably lush. We had arrived in the area after dark, and I still vividly recall the initial splendor, stepping out into sunshine and beholding an emerald field of sugar cane. "This is life!" I thought. Had I been dead all winter?

Then after a few days, I boarded a plane to come home. The day was clear, and from my window seat I watched the planet's surface below. So incredibly green as we took off and circled the city, then more tentatively green as we headed north. By Iowa, I could see snowy patches: Dorothy returning to Kansas.

Doesn't it seem odd that we live in such a narrow band of the electromagnetic spectrum? Even discounting the large part of the output that bounces back into space, those waves around 5,400 angstroms are a pretty small minority of the wavelength world. Yet we are so enmeshed in greenness that we hardly think how strange this must be. To us, to almost all animals, greenness is life, greenness is food and protection and nest material. Greenness means plants, the essential Other in our lives.

There is a paradox embedded in this green world. What seems profligacy—so much green—is actually efficiency. Green is one of the few wavelengths that plants do not use. Green light bounces off their tissues—that's why they appear green.

The ecosystems of the earth run on sunlight. It is the ability of green plants to take the sun's radiant energy and change it into other forms that makes the great web of life possible. Our human bodies, all other animal bodies, run on the fuel of food, measured in calories, and ultimately made by plants.

The wavelengths that plants use to produce this fuel are the blues and reds, and to a lesser extent, the yellows and oranges. A complex series of chemical reactions in green plants forms the sugars, proteins, and fats that are the basis of all food, and plants have evolved an array of different reactions, each utilizing different wavelengths. High school biology students study this process of photosynthesis in such detail that it makes some run screaming from the room. In a tenth grade class, it is one of the most intricate and challenging of units, an introduction to the detailed chemical mesh that undergirds life on earth.

While the green August world outside my window appears varied, with its many hues, it actually masks far more complexity. What lies beneath those verdant leaves is minutely organized. Life is tightly fitted to its planet, our earth, and the planet's tilt and its distance from the sun.

All the greenness that meets my eye this summer day is

contained in only one type of biological molecule: chloro-phyll. There are several different variations of this large mol-ecule, and these variations are useful in categorizing the plant kingdom and determining the relationships between plant groups. Chlorophyll is sensitive to blue and red light and undergoes physical change when these wavelengths hit it. In a series of intricate reactions, the energy of the sunlight is used to form simple sugar—glucose—which in turn is the basis for manufacturing proteins, fats, starch, and the nucleic acids of the genetic code. Every creature of earth is com-posed of these compounds and only these. We are all chil-dren of the sun.

In green plants, the chlorophyll doesn't meander free-form in cells but is contained in specific little structures called chloroplasts. Chloroplasts are big—you can see them under a microscope—and they also house the molecules that make proteins and fats. A single cell in a green leaf may possess forty to fifty. Chloroplasts are a novelty among cell struc-tures. They contain DNA, a molecule usually only found in the cell nucleus, and that chloroplastic DNA is very similar to the form of DNA found in bacteria. In addition, chloro-plast function is interrupted by antibiotics like streptomycin, just like bacteria. Because of this, and other similarities, biol-ogists have come to propose that the chloroplasts in green plants have evolved from free-living bacteria.

Or, in broader terms, some bacteria long ago invaded certain cells and set up shop. They kept their ability to con-vert sunlight to make sugars, and this was very useful to their host cells. The bacteria, on the other hand, gained some protection from the extremes of hot and cold weather and drought. This kind of win-win relationship in biology is termed "symbiosis," and it enabled the partners to invade land and new aquatic environments.

So green plants are a kind of evolutionary amalgam, cobbled together and immensely successful. Surely the wash of green outside my window attests to that.

Sometimes the awe is lost in a basin of murky water. I forget the wonder contained in the intricacy of chloroplasts and their chlorophyll. Pioneer Lake, too, is caught in the green season. Though never crystalline, its water progresses from a somewhat clear condition at ice-out in April to a rich, grassy color at midsummer. This change is entirely due to the growth of algal populations, fed by the abundant nutrients, chiefly phosphorus, contained in the lake. The source of this compound can be found adjacent to the lake: in fertilized lawns.

In the main, these algae—which some classify as bacteria—are not closely related to green plants but have their own category, "blue-greens." They are notorious for their slimy outer coating, which resembles mucus, and often emit an unpleasant odor. They frequently form masses that float on the water's surface. Pioneer harbors a garden variety of blue-green, *Oscillatoria,* which is slender and threadlike, visible to the naked eye. Under a microscope, I can detect green structures packed inside the filament—the organism's DNA not contained in a chloroplast.

Some of Pioneer's algae are marked by regular spirals, the chlorophyll coiling up like a very small slinky. Others are colonial, clumped together, clustered in a gelatinous mass. Some have architectural beauty; others are unlovely. Most float. In my sample jar, I note a fuzzy green mat of algal life on top of the water; beneath, the liquid is fairly clear.

Pioneer will remain green until the first frost marks the end of the growing season. As the waters cool in the fall,

algal growth will taper off. In November I will again look at
the bottom of the lake through three feet of water.

On the last Sunday in August, I sit in my pew at church and
gaze out the side door of the sanctuary, which is open wide
to the summer morning. An American redstart has sung in
the fringe of trees across the road through June and July.
Now, in late summer, the breeding season is over, and he is
probably busy feeding fledglings. I think I might be able to
hear his warbler "chip" in the nearby bushes, though.

My family and I sit in the same pew each Sunday, not
only because we are Lutheran and Lutherans like predict-
ability and order, but because I can look out the open door
and watch the activity on the bank above North Center
Lake. Sitting so close to the outdoors, there is a blurring of
sacred and secular space. It is not clear where one ends and
the other begins. Sometimes a cooling breeze wafts off the
water and finds its way into the sanctuary.

This morning, I observe several dead trees on the edge
of the road, on the crest of the lakeshore. I am sure these
trees were alive in June. They're elms, small elms, and they
have succumbed to another assault by Dutch elm disease.
This fungus from Europe swept through the Midwest in a
fury four decades ago, decimating the native American elm.
In the years following, it has returned for the scattered individuals it somehow missed. Every summer we see one or
two local elms yellow prematurely, drop leaves, and die,
another casualty to the fungal attack.

Dutch elm, ash yellows, cedar apple rust, white pine
blister rust, oak wilt. A plethora of diseases conspire to dull
the freshness of the green season. Recently, I learned of a new
disease, sapstreak, which threatens the sugar maple, the

dominant tree in our local woods. Secretly, I had exulted that this one tree, at least, was free from threat. No longer.

I turn my attention to inside the sanctuary, where green paraments adorn the ornately carved altar, the pulpit, and lectern. Golden stalks of embroidered wheat wave their seed heads from the richly colored tapestries. They complement the stenciled purple grape design that decorates the chancel arch. Together they are meant to symbolize bread and wine, but in this initial representation they are not "processed" but elemental: green plants, wheat grass and grapevine. They are delegates from the natural world to the sacred realm. They are emissaries with a message: the Body and the Blood, the bread and the wine, the grape and the wheat, and you— human beings—we are one with you. There is a fundamental, if unconscious, sensibility of ecological relationship here.

The Sundays after Pentecost, so-called Ordinary Time, are also known as the Green Season. The paraments reflect this. All the Sundays in summer, when the landscape is resplendent with chlorophyll-laden plants, belong to the green season. The color was chosen early in the history of the Church to depict life, and growth and hope.

I'll admit that I need this word of *hope* at times when I catch sight of dead trees in the middle of summer, or encounter algal-riddled waters. My spirit flags when I mull over environmental ills. We tend to take summer's vitality for granted, when in actuality it is just one prolonged drought, or disease, away from decimation.

I do rely on Christianity's hope, although I also cringe to voice the thought. So many have sought refuge in a simplistic belief in a Heaven that has no ties to this green planet and have used the idea as an excuse not to concern themselves with its ill-treatment. But rightly understood, this religion is not a refuge for the cowardly or inattentive but a cradle for the courageous, who spring from it to confront the ills of this world. For me, in this time of climate change, there is no other green space that nurtures. Surely I can't rest on the track record of the human race in rising to the occasion to address looming catastrophe.

Once, a simple walk in a park or the woods was enough to nourish me completely. It still can refresh me, but it has become harder and harder to ignore what I take as ominous signs: not one Swainson's thrush in a spring forest, not one spring peeper calling from an ephemeral pond, only a handful of monarch butterflies migrating south when ten years ago I saw hundreds.

And so, to the last refuge, the one with the ancient words, the one holding out hope in the grimmest of times.

I have long been intrigued by the assignation of color to emotional state. "I just saw red!" a furious friend exclaims. "It's golden!" my son says with satisfaction. There are black moods and blue days, yellow bellies and white feathers. We seem to take from the color green a mixed message. Someone might be green with envy, or merely nauseous, green around the gills. Sometimes green people are the inexperienced. At other times, they are those striving to be environmentally correct.

Being green may be a passing stage, on the way to ripeness. Or it may mean being exceptionally fresh and vital, like the succulent vegetables at a green grocer's.

I say yes to all of these, to the complexity of those alive to the green season. We are both inexperienced and fresh. We long for growth and vitality. We are ill with the state of the earth. We listen for the green hope pregnant in the small voice that whispers to us that this, too, might be saved.

# Rowing the Mutant Canoe

W aiting for us at the edge of Pioneer Lake, at the foot of our dock, is an odd sort of watercraft, perhaps unique in the entire Chisago Lakes area. As a biologist, I might term it a *chimera*—that is, a misfit organism of two genetically distinct parents. It is a creature that doesn't occur naturally. Chimeras are usually forced into being through the active imagination of a human being, say, through laboratory manipulation.

Our Pioneer chimera is a canoe that can be rowed as a scull. My husband has taken out the middle thwart of our seventeen-foot Old Town canoe and replaced it with a contraption of aluminum tubing and padded webbing. In one position, it serves as a central seat for a rower. When flipped around, it becomes a cushy portage yoke for resting the craft on the shoulders. In addition, he has affixed a second contrivance, labeled by its manufacturer as a "rowing outrigger," directly aft of the added seat/yoke. This gadget, also constructed of aluminum for lightness and strength, clamps to the gunwales of the canoe and provides a place to position the oarlocks that hold the oars propelling the chimera through the water.

The oars are the remaining elements of the scull parentage of our fantastical creature. They are wholly unlike our trusty canoe paddles, and not even remotely similar to the clunky wooden oars I plied as a child. These propellants sport "spoon blades" at their termini, which are cupped, similar to kayak paddles. Their manufacturer claims that they "hold the water" thirty-one inches of a stroke. I presume this means that if one measured the arc of a stroke from start to finish, thirty-one inches of its length would be in the water. While it seems strange that someone would describe an oar in this way, this quality seems somehow fitting for a chimera, a quirky invention to begin with.

Our family is fond of its canoes. They provide a chief form of activity during the months of open water. We haul them off to streams and rivers near and far on pleasant summer days. It is a little unsettling to me to walk down to the lake and see our beloved green Old Town gussied up in aluminum contrivances, clamped and screwed and braced along its length. I pat its sleek Royalex flank: that's OK, that's OK, I murmur. We'll take you to the Boundary Waters, too.

The birth of our chimera is a convoluted tale. It begins nearly thirty years ago, when my husband and I lived in St. Paul and bicycled along the Mississippi River each day on our way to the university. On early mornings, we'd glimpse a rowing team out on the water and admire the swift sleekness of the sculls as they glided past, the coxswain calling out the rhythm. Such an elegant activity. Tom especially was taken with the sport.

Years passed. We settled on the shores of Pioneer, grew to middle age, and became restless. There's something about turning forty that rekindles old attractions. A reflective soul thinks, "I have a limited amount of time left here. I'd like to do this . . ." Tom thought being the owner of a single-person scull would be a fine way to enjoy his middle years. He justified his yearning by considering it an excellent way to exercise and maintain upper body strength. A competitive swimmer, he was finding it difficult to get to the local pool on a regular basis. A scull on Pioneer would be so convenient and had the added attraction of being an outdoor activity.

When he went online to price out the elegant, high-tech craft, however, he blanched. A single-person scull could be had for two thousand dollars. Even when in the grip of mid-life yearning, he thought that too extravagant an indulgence. Cruising on the Internet, Tom stumbled on an alternative possibility, something truly "other." A small, family-owned company based on Minnesota's Iron Range offered canoe and kayak "accessories." Now, these were not accessories one normally considers for such boats—paddles, seats. These were wildly creative and designed to meet needs only dedicated canoeists might hanker for, while enduring a mile-long portage or a headwind down a very long lake. They included more comfortable yokes for carrying canoes on the shoulders, backrests for aging vertebral columns, sails that attach to kayaks with suction cups, and gizmos for attaching these watercraft to cars and trucks. (They also make whimsical items. A pet life vest, for example, for eighteen dollars, is designed for dogs that travel by boat. A catalogue photo shows a vest modeled by Freddie, a sad-looking Bassett hound.)

It is hard not to imagine a mad, creative inventor tucked away in tiny Mountain Iron, Minnesota (population 2,981), thinking up one notion after another, to meet all the complaints paddlers voice after a day on the water. Our "Rowing Unit" is one such invention. It extends a canoe's pivot points by placing the oarlocks on aluminum rods about twelve inches beyond the gunwales, the sides of the watercraft. This essentially makes the canoe's narrow hull functionally wider, more like a rowboat. The canoe acquires, then, the power and stability of a rowboat, when rowed like one.

The company, Spring Creek, touts the superior speed of

rowing a canoe. "One person can easily keep up with two," the catalogue claims. Rowing also enhances a canoe's maneuverability: "[It can] turn on a dime and handle a blowing wind." The rowing unit with paddles cost $257. Tom thought he could venture that sum to experiment with Spring Creek's offering. He plunked his money down and soon our seventeen-foot Old Town, the family's most-used canoe, assumed a new identity.

The rowing unit does everything as promised. The canoe feels stable on the water. Most days we row without life vests. One good pull on an oar swings the craft around. And above all, it is fast. For paddlers used to puttering leisurely along at the rate of three miles per hour, rowing a canoe feels like traveling at warp speed. The backyards fly by. In no time, a rower reaches the far shore and must whip the canoe around.

Each summer, the Center City Historical Society holds a canoe race on North Center Lake as part of the July Center City Days festival. Each year, we study the race announcement carefully. No more than two people can be in a racing canoe. (How about one person?) Paddlers must wear approved life jackets. (What, we think, can rowers wear?) One participant must be at least sixteen years old. (We qualify there.) There is no rule concerning a canoe with less than two people, and nothing banning additional, nonmotorized equipment. Unacquainted with canoe/scull chimeras, the Historical Society seems to have given us rowers an opening.

Each year we gleefully consider entering the green canoe in the race, imagining a quick trip down lake to the turnaround point in the race. We fantasize about how discombobulated the judges (who are friends of ours) would be when Tom appears with the mutant, clearly unconventional and clearly faster than the other canoes. We have yet to enter our chimera, however. After all, we're known in this town. Neighbors could get even any number of ways.

On a melancholy morning in September, I slip down the path to the lake, intent on spending time on the water. Change is in the offing. The kids went back to school on Tuesday; the summer's haphazard schedule has given way to days meted out in school bells, tennis meets, and after-school rehearsals.

Nature, too, is coming off the summer life. Small greenish warblers, migrating south, skulk through the wood's understory, foraging for insects. A cold front went through last night, and we had rain before breakfast. Now the world is damp and soggy, the air heavy with cloying humidity. It was ninety degrees yesterday, and though the front has brought some relief, it is still overwarm for September. If Septembers must be melancholic, I would like them to be cool. I'd rather be pensive snuggled into a flannel shirt and jeans than uncomfortably sweaty in shorts and a tank top. But summer temperatures seem to linger longer and longer these days.

The mutant canoe is resting on blocks on its gunwales. It seems exhausted after a summer of fun. I flip it over, push it off into the shoreline grasses, and ease the stern into the water. A moment later I am perched on the central seat, trying to figure out which oar goes into what oarlock. I solve that puzzle, then, one pull, two, and I'm clear of the dock. Another sweep brings me out into open water. I point the bow in the direction of the church and, facing aft, begin to row in earnest. The physical activity of rowing embodies the paradox of moving forward by looking backward, and it is a fitting metaphor for this morning. I need to bring my sensibilities into the approaching autumn, but first, one last look at the all-too-fleeting summer.

Bring the oars back, lean the torso forward, draw the blades through the water, and pull, pull. I learned to row a boat in childhood, and the motion brings with it overtones of my youth. The creak of the oarlocks is the same, and the glide, and the astonishing feeling of speed over water.

Today will not be an outing for ferreting out small birds or late-blooming asters. Today will be a morning devoted to shaking off the blues. Pull, pull! The far shore looms, and with two quick turns of my right oar I swing the bow around and aim now for the northern edge of Pioneer, half a mile away.

Pull, pull! Now the church recedes with each stroke. Pull, pull! Past the summer docks, where pontoons are tied, evoking memories of the warm evenings in August. Pull, pull! Past the courthouse, past the terraced yard, past the water-ski course, past our own dock reaching out into the water. Looking backward, always looking backward at where I have been.

The last of the summer's pink joe-pye weed is fading at the shore. Up ahead, glancing over my shoulder, I see there's a sumac aflame with one red leaf, and now I am flying, flying, flying into autumn.

# Ordinary Time

I remember learning to tell time. Our square red-and-white kitchen clock with the art deco numerals was my model. It sat on the kitchen counter next to the stove for decades, a testimony to a marriage made in 1950 and to my parents' parsimony in preserving household goods. I was five, on the cusp of kindergarten, ready to leave the timeless days of family life behind and enter the real world of school schedules and dismissal bells. My mother must have considered the ability to tell time a survival skill.

The hour hand was thick and sluggish, like a dumpy person or an especially fat pickle. The minute hand, slender and agile, actually could be seen to move and seemed to direct its ponderous cousin forward. I grasped the concept quickly, though there was a leap of translation involved: when the long hand points to the 3, call it fifteen, and when it points to the 6, it is actually thirty. Once I figured out the code, I was forever changed. Now time progressed in orderly, describable fashion, one minute after another, the thin directive minute hand pushing the hour hand into the future, around and around the face of the clock.

Nearly everyone wears a wristwatch these days. In addition to my faithful Pulsar, I have eight clocks in my house, including one on the stove and one on the microwave. My husband and I keep two in our bedroom, one (mine) an old-fashioned analog connected to a radio that brings me chatty news in the morning, and one (his) a high-tech digital that is reset automatically for accuracy in accordance with a "mother clock" in Boulder, Colorado.

We are so utterly conditioned to think of time as being meted out in equal durations of seconds, minutes, and hours in modern life, and we are so busy rushing about, making the most of it, that we have nearly lost the capacity to consider time in other ways. Past societies, however, have not run about with wristwatches permanently attached, and people nonetheless fell in love and married, mated and formed children, enjoyed a glass of wine and a good story, sickened and died. Vestiges of this past world, before the pervasive presence of chronometers, are everywhere, just lurking beneath the veneer of modernity.

The people in the yellow brick church observe the passage of time by a different calendar, the liturgical year. Most of the Christian liturgical year, the seasons that conjure up evocative images of Christmas trees, or Easter lilies, wreaths with candles or crosses swathed in black, falls into Sacred Time. Sacred Time is concerned with the divine acts of Incarnation and Resurrection and lends itself to dramatic gesture. Church services are intense and might reach for the viscera. But humans cannot live forever under intensity, and there is another part to the liturgical year. In the long, sunny days of summer and into the golden harvest, the great expanse of Sundays—those falling between the celebration of Pentecost, when the disciples received "tongues of fire," and the first flame of Advent—is termed "ordinary." The season is simply Ordinary Time.

Church scholars are quick to point out that Ordinary Time comes not from a meaning of "commonplace" or "mundane" but, rather, from the root word *ordinal*—counted time. The Sundays in Ordinary Time are marked off in orderly fashion: First Sunday after Pentecost, Second Sunday after Pentecost, and so on, all the way up to the Twenty-Seventh Sunday after Pentecost in some years. But *ordinary* and *ordinal* do have the same root and share the same sense of expectation: nothing unpredictable or out of the ordinary will happen. Jesus tells parables, delivers sermons, and issues warnings in the Gospel lessons of Ordinary Time, but he generally stays within the laws of nature. The miracles are reserved for the season of Epiphany.

When I was a child, sitting through the July heat of Sunday sermons and interminable prayers, the Sundays after Pentecost seemed much like the summer days encompassing them: endless and unchanging. The green altar cloth remained in place. You could count on its verdant color and its intertwining three circles representing the Trinity, and the three wavy lines of water on which sailed a rowboat, the ship of the Church. The liturgy never varied, we sang generic hymns of praise and thanksgiving (no Christmas carols). It was, oh god, so boring, so ordinary.

I once agreed to give a chapel talk to my alma mater, a short message, six or seven minutes long at most. I had been invited to speak to a general biology class on environmental organizations and had offered to speak in chapel. I immediately regretted it. No sooner had the chaplain accepted my offer than I felt I had been audacious, overly bold, maybe even egotistical. I wished devoutly that I could wiggle out of the commitment and knew just as surely that I was going to have to deliver that homily.

As I drove through the southern Minnesota countryside to the college that morning, I felt acutely tuned to the rhythms of the small communities I passed. At one intersection, I saw children clutching backpacks, waiting for the school bus. At another, I watched a bus driver put on her flashing red lights, extend the no-passing arm, and usher a small child on board. There was a tank truck winding up a side road, collecting milk from dairy farmers; there was a driver wearing a green John Deere cap, in a pickup pulling a grain wagon, bringing in a load of bright corn to the local mill. All of these people were living in ordinary time, while I was yanked out of my normal routine, in an apprehensive turn of mind that seemed extraordinary and uncomfortable. If I was not in Ordinary Time, was I in Sacred Time? I can tell you, I did not feel holy.

I think wistfully of ordinary time on days when I am destined to attend a funeral. While I thread nylon stockings over my toes and up my legs, slip on a black dress and maybe a jacket, I think of all the people starting the day in comfortable clothing—jeans or corduroys, sweaters and knit shirts. I long for ordinary time during periods of sadness, when I have the leisure to examine the minutes but not the energy to fill them. Ordinary time abandons me in times of intensity, too: I call to mind my four long spells of labor leading up to childbirth, in which time progressed not by a mechanical chronometer but by nature itself, in waves of contractions, which I counted by rhythmic breathing, massage, and little puffs of blown-out air.

Later, these children I birthed gave me glimpses of eternity—not necessarily pleasant ones—when we faced midnight matches with the croup, the child barking like a seal and gasping for breath, or again, under the glaze of a 105-degree fever, with flushed skin and filmy eyes, when I'd think, "Surely this child will not live to see daybreak." Sacred time cuts close to the bone, often exposing that thin, barely decipherable distinction between life and death. That is why the weeks surrounding Christmas and Easter are distinguished from Ordinary Time. For what do the Incarnation and the Resurrection speak to if not birth and death?

This past summer, I marked time on Pioneer Lake by observing the wood duck family. Wood ducks are birds graced with extravagant beauty. The drake is brightly colored with a ruby eye and emerald head ending in an exotic tail. They are confiding little creatures that, like robins, are not particularly secretive about family matters. They are cavity nesters and once nested exclusively in dead trees, often in holes carved out by woodpeckers. Such trees are in short supply these days, and happily, the birds have adapted to the artificial cavities of nest boxes that sympathetic humans provide. That people have done so is one reason that we have wood ducks on Pioneer Lake today. The loss of natural nest sites, as people removed "unsightly" dead trees, hurt the wood duck population.

The wood duck's story, however, is sadder than habitat loss. The species was nearly driven into extinction by overhunting. Wood ducks were once bountiful and before the Migratory Bird Treaty of 1918 were hunted without restraint. Daily bag limits of up to six hundred were not uncommon, and this thoughtless killing took its toll. At the turn of the past century, wood ducks were scarce, and there were probably none on our lake. In 1918, with the passage of legislation, the hunting season closed on wood ducks, and for the next twenty-two years they were strictly off limits. With the hunting pressure off, the birds made a remarkable recovery, and once again it is legal to hunt them. They are, in fact, the third most common duck hunted in Minnesota.

We have a wood duck box in the alder thicket on the

north end of the lake. It provides a suitable spot for Pioneer's wood ducks to begin a family. The birds arrive after ice-out and lay their eggs in April. Bird-watchers who erect and keep an eye on nest boxes sometimes record the day the eggs are laid. They count thirty days to hatching. Then, within twenty-four hours the newly hatched ducklings will leave their box to begin life on the water with their mother.

Nest boxes are often eight to ten feet above the water—or, sometimes, the hard, hard ground—but the young ducklings leap out of their own accord to reach the water, which harbors their food. They have been measured dropping from trees as tall as 290 feet: skyscraper proportions! And the feat lends itself to spectators. Minnesota bird-watchers have been known to host "coming out" parties, where the guests gather to (discreetly) witness the event and sip champagne.

Pioneer's wood ducks were a little slow to start their family this year. Perhaps a predator had eaten the first eggs, and they had to renest. By mid-July, however, the young ducklings appeared with their mother on the south end of the lake. (Drakes don't hang around after the eggs hatch.)

Wood ducks are known for their ability to proliferate. Broods can number as many as fifteen ducklings, but parentage is complicated by the tendency for one female to dump her eggs in another's nest box. This leaves some poor, distracted mother to tend large numbers of ducklings, at least for a while. The mortality rate is high for young birds. This seemed true for our ducklings. Pedaling my bike past the south end of the lake one morning, I counted ten ducklings in a row behind the mother, paddling furiously. A few days later, I saw only nine, and a week after that, the brood was down to seven. Even on little Pioneer Lake, life is perilous. Several sizeable snapping turtles call the lake home, a raccoon family holes up in the parsonage woods on the east shore, and great horned owls and red foxes frequent the area—all interested in making a meal out of a duckling.

By August, though, the predation dropped off, and I regularly saw the duck and her seven offspring drifting along the south end. Juvenile wood ducks resemble the female, and as the family grew bigger it was often difficult to distinguish the mother from her teenaged young.

I never cease relying on a calendar to number my precious summer days, but wood ducks, if they have any sense of time passing, exist forever not in counted time but in some other kind, perhaps in God's time. Their clock is the heartbeat of the physical world—the pulse of chemical reactions that form muscle, bone, blood, and feathers, the rhythm of which takes a measured thirty days from fertilized egg to hatchling. The hatchling, impelled not by a wristwatch but by some inner urge, abandons the protection of the nest before two nights have passed.

Life, death, life, death. The ducklings grow, their numbers dwindle, the small prey they eat also increase in size and number. The distinction between nature's time and sacred time seems blurred.

In September, I noticed the wood ducks had returned to the northern end of the lake, to the protection of the alder thicket. I often saw them perched on a long, half-submerged log as I rowed on foggy fall mornings. Their soft, taupe-colored feathers blended into the fading vegetation. They always plopped gently into the water when they caught sight of my boat. They stayed together, all seven with their mother, and I'm pretty sure that's where they were last Sunday morning when, on the first dawn of duck hunting, gunshots ripped open the tranquil morning air.

There is another way to think about time, other than as ordinary or sacred. The ancient Greeks distinguished between *chronos* and *kairos,* a distinction of great significance in the New Testament of the Bible, written as it was in Greek. *Chronos* is measured time, time that is ticked off by the swinging of a pendulum or the measure of a second hand. The Bible sometimes refers to time in this way, but the predominant way of thinking about time is as *kairos. Kairos* is a time of opportunity or of fulfillment. *Kairos* is a Greek word, found in the New Testament, but the Hebrew Old Testament has an equivalent word, *'eth,* the meaning of which permeates its pages, including the familiar passage from Ecclesiastes:

> For everything there is a season, and a time for every
>     matter under heaven:
> A time to be born and a time to die;
> A time to plant and a time to pluck up what is planted;
> A time to kill and a time to heal;
> A time to break down and a time to build up;
> A time to weep and a time to laugh;
> A time to mourn and a time to dance.

An understanding of *kairos* is more pointed in the New Testament. The Gospel writer Mark launches Christ on his ministry with these words: "The time is fulfilled and the kingdom of God is at hand." It is the time of opportunity. I have never seen an understanding of *kairos* applied to the natural world, but it seems to me that all of nature measures time only by *kairos* and never by *chronos.*

A pair of wood ducks arrives on Pioneer shortly after the vernal equinox, when sunlight is increasing and daily warmth has broken the winter's ice. They had selected partners in the short days of winter, but the time had not been right, in winter, to lay eggs. In spring, though, on a northern lake, the suitable season presents itself. The birds mate and nest. There is enough food in the awakening ecosystem of the lake to sustain a duck that expends tremendous energy making yolk-laden eggs. The eggs hatch when the shells can no longer contain growing ducklings, and the ducklings make the great leap out of the nest cavity when its space can no longer contain all their fuzzy bodies.

All of summer is a time of opportunity to grow and mature because all the creatures of the lake are seizing the chance provided by long days of abundant sunshine and its hospitable warmth. Green plants capture the sun's energy and make sugars. Small aquatic animals nibble the plants or graze on green algae, getting bigger and producing offspring themselves. Summer is the time of fulfillment, when the promise of a fertilized egg comes into fruition.

Then comes autumn, as the earth on its axis tilts the Northern Hemisphere away from the sun and the auspicious hour of reproduction ends. It opens on another purpose: to prepare to endure the winter, or to leave altogether and sit out the season in warmer climes. For our Pioneer ducks, fall brings less beneficent days, as I witnessed last weekend, the time to be hunted. Acting strictly on *chronos*—a date set by the Department of Natural Resources—humans seize the occasion to pursue wild game as our ancestors did. But in truth, we are long past the time when we could ever act naturally in the natural world. Our human numbers are too high, duck numbers too low, and their habitat too slight for us to ever again be unselfconscious predators.

Nevertheless, the natural world has bounty for us. To live in *kairos,* as other earthlings do, is to work in harmony with the world. Many hunters would say that is why they are out in the marshes in the chill dawn with shotguns in their hands. They are resetting their internal clocks, an annual undertaking, to fit themselves properly into the biological world, to become part of a natural food chain once more.

I am not a hunter of game, but I am a gatherer of clues. I look for the proper time in which to launch ideas, I wait for the time of fulfillment in which they will ripen and produce fruit. We fool ourselves with our clocks and watches, thinking we can harness time. We will always fail. Time unfolds by its own inner workings.

# Nighthawk Day

The great vortex undulated above my head, alive with the forms and flutter of birds. In the rosy light of a setting sun, I could make out the irregular wing beat of chimney swifts, their dark silhouettes as compact as little bullets, but there was a second bird in the whirlwind, swirling with the swifts. Penetrating the rapid chitter of the swift could be heard the nasal "peent" of common nighthawks, and in the dimming light I detected their angular wings, each marked with a single white bar.

I encountered this spectacular spiral of birds while on an early September walk around Pioneer Lake. The evenings were growing cooler and shorter, and I moved briskly to make it home before sunset, when I was brought up short by the cacophony of bird voices and looked up to see the spiral rising into the clear sky.

A mere taste of a sweet madeleine opened a well of memory for Marcel Proust in *Remembrance of Things Past*. My memory unlocks with a single "peent" of a nighthawk. I hear its cry and am immediately transported back to my college days, when the birds encircled the tall steeple of the chapel at dusk. The prairie wind had quieted at the end of a breezy day, and I listened to the nighthawks as I walked from my dorm to the library or from the library to the canteen for coffee.

Thirty years ago, nighthawks were also common in our

St. Paul neighborhood. Their distinctive, unmusical buzz filled the air on evening walks down shady streets past the neatly kept houses of Merriam Park. In town, in the country, on the edge of the prairie, common nighthawks are birds well suited for the presence of humans and their settlements. Their diet consists of common insects, and they lay their eggs, without benefit of a nest, on flat surfaces, including gravel roofs.

I was happy to see nighthawks swooping and diving around the steeple of the yellow brick church when we first came to Center City, a short thirteen years ago. One of the pleasures of middle age is the deep layering of experience, and each "peent" of a nighthawk brought with it a collage of my past.

But nighthawks disappeared from Pioneer Lake soon after we came. What had been common became, in short succession, rare and then nonexistent. Their absence created one more hole in the avian presence, but in a distracting and distractible world, holes are not widely noticed. I missed the nighthawks, yes, but did not anguish over them—until I encountered this mass of migrating birds. The whirling spiral that now rotated over my head was the largest number of nighthawks I had seen in decades.

Where did they go?

Nighthawks are aerial feeders, rushing from midair to nab insects on the wing. They feast on June bugs, potato beetles, mosquitoes, and grasshoppers, many of which people consider pests, leading Minnesota ornithologist T. S. Roberts to consider the nighthawk "one of our most valuable birds." It is this tendency to feed on the wing, entirely on insects, that has led the Minnesota Ornithologists' Union to consider the common nighthawk a species at risk, although it is not listed by federal or state government as endangered or threatened. Its nocturnal habit also precludes it from being detected on Breeding Bird Surveys, which are generally run in early morning, so its population trends are not closely monitored.

But one doesn't need a count or data sheet to know that the once-plentiful common nighthawk has suffered a long and drastic decline in numbers. This trend started decades ago, before the age of widespread pesticide use. Even in 1932, Roberts, writing in *The Birds of Minnesota*, observed that the bird was "much less numerous" as a nesting bird in the state, even though it had never been hunted, and its habitat was apparently intact. In Roberts's day, however, nighthawks still commanded a dramatic presence in the fall skies. As Canada's vast population migrated through Minnesota, "hundreds and hundreds" of birds lazily circled and swooped over Minnesota's forests and lakes, feeding on insects as they kept a steady drift southward. Roberts termed days when the air was thick with birds "Nighthawk Days." He described a particular late August evening at Itasca State Park when "the air was filled with a great whirling mass of birds, feeding on flying insects" and added he had once driven east to west across the entire breadth of Minnesota without a break in nighthawks. Earlier observers in the 1800s numbered the birds in the "thousands and thousands" in early September Nighthawk Days. Roberts's account pales by comparison.

I did not know any of this when I came upon the whirling vortex on Pioneer Lake's shore, or I would have seen it for what it really was: the thin ghost of a once-stupendous event, a faint echo fading into oblivion. I haven't seen one since.

Not long after the spectacular spiral, I was again out for an evening walk, and this time I came upon a single wounded nighthawk on the southern shore of the lake, just below the church hill. The bird hobbled about frantically, unable to fly, its right wing held at an awkward angle. I suspected it had encountered a car while single-mindedly pursuing insects that hovered over the water. The result was a broken wing.

I hadn't seen any nighthawks in the days since the spiral, so this bird must have been a straggling migrant from farther north. How distressing for the bird to have come this far only to be injured. The nighthawk was quite feisty, hissing loudly when I approached. I took this as a good sign. Perhaps its only injury was the wing. I took off my jacket and threw it over the bird, then scooped it gently into my arms and took it home.

Common nighthawks are attractive birds. They are members of the Goatsucker family (named for the erroneous belief that the birds got milk from the udders of goats), and like their cousins, the whippoorwills, they possess distinctive adaptive features. I had never seen one up close before, and I now peeked at the feathery creature under my jacket. I first noticed its wide, gaping mouth, almost like that of a frog, which it could hold open as it flew for insects. The eyes were unusually large, dark round buttons, good for night vision. Tiny sensory whiskers around its beak enhanced its ability to detect flying insects. Its brown feathers seemed especially fluffy, almost fur-like.

Once home, I settled the bird in an old laundry basket padded with a towel and covered it so it wouldn't escape. I then started calling around in an attempt to find a wildlife rehabilitator who could help. An Audubon friend directed me to the Wildlife Rehabilitation Center in Roseville as the only possible source of aid that night. Roseville, a northern suburb of St. Paul, is forty-five miles away, and I inwardly groaned, thinking I'd have to drive into the Cities that evening. The rehab center, however, assured me that the bird would most likely survive until the next day and instructed me to put it in a shoebox to completely confine the wing, and to not attempt to give it any food or water. My family spent the remainder of the evening speaking in low tones and tiptoeing around.

The night passed and the next morning as I peered under the lid of the shoebox, I was greeted by a defiant hiss. Okay, good, I thought. On to rehab. The Wildlife Rehabilitation Center is adjacent to the Harriet Alexander Nature Center in the midst of Roseville's Central Park. A modest but substantial building, the center was begun in 1976 by some veterinary students at the University of Minnesota. Entirely dependent on donations, it has become an established institution. Three-fourths of all wildlife in Minnesota that have been successfully treated and released back into the environment pass through its doors. Patients have included deer, raccoons, all kinds of birds, and even snakes.

When we entered and I handed the shoebox and its occupant over to the nurse, I was given a patient information form to fill out: type of animal, when found, cause of injury (witnessed? assumed?). I felt like I was admitting one of my own children. The feeling intensified as I was given a second clipboard informing me of how the center receives its funding, and would I care to make a donation? Suddenly, *the* nighthawk had become *my* nighthawk, and I realized that it was incumbent upon me to pay for its care—even though all indications were that the bird was not appreciative.

The receptionist told me that they had several nighthawks convalescing at the center and that if the wing could be set and healed, the bird would be released in an appropriate flock of migrants to continue its journey south. When I had finished filling out the forms, the receptionist handed me a little card with a quote from the naturalist Henry Beston:

> We need another and a wiser and perhaps a more mystical concept of animals. Remote from universal nature, and living by complicated artifice, man in civilization surveys the creature through the glass of his knowledge and sees thereby a feather magnified and the whole image in distortion. We patronize them for their incompleteness, for their tragic fate of having taken form so far below ourselves. And therein we err, and greatly err. For the animal shall not be measured by man. In a world older and more complete than ours, they move finished and complete, gifted with extensions of the senses we have lost or never attained, living by voices we shall never hear. They are not brethren, they are not underlings; they are other nations, caught with ourselves in the net of life, fellow prisoners of the splendor and travail of the earth.
>
> (*The Outermost House*, 1928)

I left the Rehab Center relieved that my nighthawk was in good, capable hands. So often I see animals suffer and am utterly helpless to act. I decided that the pleasure in caring for the bird had been all mine.

We patch up the world one nighthawk at a time.

# Via Dolorosa

O n the first day of summer vacation this year, as we approached the driveway into our cabin, we came upon the porcupine that lived under our front steps, dead on the highway. Its quills were raised, the brown fur glossy and stiff beneath them, and I could see its rounded nose and perfect paws. Porcupines are slow, bumbling creatures and take a long time to cross a road. Though the speed limit is fifty-five miles per hour on our highway, people go seventy.

If I ever go certifiably around the bend, it will be because of roadkill.

This is a frightening thought because roadkill is part of daily life in a technological society. It is the cost of "doing business." It is collateral damage. To thrive in such a world as ours, a sane person needs to don emotional armor as protection against the slaughter laid bare on the roads every day. I seem unable to do this, however, and consequently each time I step out onto an asphalt strip, I sense how emotionally fragile I am, how ill equipped to be an American. As Americans go, I am at high risk for sensitivity to roadkill because I engage in two activities: as a bird-watcher, I am acutely attuned to the avian residents in my neighborhood; and as a fitness runner, I am in earthy contact with miles of roadway on a daily basis.

This June, there were bobolinks nesting in a hayfield on

County 9; sedge wrens skulked all summer in thickets in certain low-lying areas along County 12. One perky kestrel staked out a portion of a particular telephone wire and appeared there each time I ran by, and an eastern bluebird held down another phone wire at the corner of County 37 and Pleasant Valley Road.

It broke my heart to discover the blue-feathered form on the verge of County 37 when out on a run two weeks ago. Thank God, the breeding season was over. No young birds depended on his presence any longer. But it's sad to know he will not migrate, or return, with all this summer's experience, to renest.

In recent weeks, I've also come upon a couple of young indigo buntings, their immature azure plumage streaked with brown. They appeared perfect, no indication of injury, save for a broken neck. You might imagine whispering at the funeral parlor, "She looks like she is sleeping." Young buntings must fly low to the ground, putting them in the path of rushing cars more so than adult birds.

Especially heartbreaking are the warblers I discover in the spring, during their two-thousand-mile odyssey from Central America. One day, I found a striking Cape May warbler, brilliant yellow with rusty cheek patches, dead at the foot of my driveway. Warblers are quick, agile sprites, but no match for an SUV. Imagine flying over the Gulf of Mexico, the rangeland of Texas, the cities of St. Louis and Kansas City, the planted cornfields of Iowa—all that way, that perilous journey, only to be killed on a Minnesota street, by someone going sixty in a forty-five-mile zone.

The pain and regret over the massacre on our roads rise from many wells. When a migrating bird is the victim, I feel a rush of sadness over the futility of heroic effort—such a small creature, flying an incredible distance, and all for naught. Sometimes the regret is bright with a sense of waste. All summer, residents in our town have been living with massive road construction on Highway 8, the interminably busy thoroughfare through our county. Thick, four-foot-high barriers have been in place since May, separating the highway from the lake and from the adjacent lanes under construction. We drive miles through a narrow concrete tunnel that essentially divides South Center from North Center Lake.

Nonetheless, the barrier is not impenetrable. Somehow, the lakes' turtles manage to enter this concrete tunnel of doom, and once in, there is no escape. Mornings, we have witnessed magnificent snapping turtles, two feet long, smashed on the pavement. Their blood is scarlet, signifying the presence of hemoglobin; they are our kin. Snapping turtles can live sixty years. How long have the venerable reptiles avoided the hazards of first being small and vulnerable, then experiencing innumerable winters, the flashing blades of outboard motors, only to die on Highway 8?

I myself have killed a handful of creatures in my thirty-five years behind a steering wheel. I think regretfully of a meadowlark that slammed into my windshield on I-90 in South Dakota, an eastern kingbird—one of a pair—that I hit while speeding on Kost Road running between North Branch and Center City, and a nocturnal cat that darted in front of my Toyota one night as I drove a babysitter home. The roadkill that rises freshest in my mind, though, is the fox squirrel that lost its life under my wheels several years back.

Fox squirrels are somewhat common in Minnesota, although most folks probably do not realize that they are a separate species from the ubiquitous gray squirrel. Fox squirrels are larger, heavier animals, with lovely rufous fur, and because they are less domesticated than their small gray cousins, I thrill every time I spy one. They are also less agile than gray squirrels, slower to check course, pivot, and spin, and perhaps they are less quick-witted as well, because each time I have hit a fox squirrel (twice), I was traveling at the speed limit and had expected the animal to wheel about and head for the shoulder of the road—but it didn't.

Still, they are small and make only a hollow thunk as they ricochet off the chassis of the car. The last one I hit collided with the car itself and wasn't run over. I cringed and clutched the wheel at the sound of impact. In my rearview mirror, its perfect, furry body lay still on the road.

It was July. I wondered if the squirrel was a mother, nursing young. If so, then this highway death would multiply. But any fox squirrel is a grievous loss. Although I have not taught biology for many years and haven't prepared a study skin for even longer, my impulse was to recover what I could from the death of the squirrel. So I pulled over, stopped the car, and went to retrieve it.

How soft the fur! Its body still warm! I lay the small animal on the floor of the car, and when I got home, slid it into a plastic bag and put it in the freezer. Surely someone, somewhere, could use a fox squirrel. It would make a fine display if mounted by a taxidermist. Even a modest study skin for a class or a mammal scientific collection would be useful.

How we fool ourselves into thinking that our actions are not as bad as they seem. That squirrel was dead, lost to its world and lost to the human world, too. No one wanted a perfect but dead fox squirrel. When I learned from a taxidermist that it would cost me at least $150 to have it prepared and mounted to display in our home, I took it out of the freezer and buried it.

Working biologists inure themselves to the heartbreak of death by focusing on populations rather than individuals.

In nature, individuals come and go, and death is a part of life; the population remains, the fundamental unit of a biological community. Most research is conducted with enough individuals in a population to get statistically significant results. Researchers seldom get to know their subjects personally, to become conversant with the quirks and idiosyncrasies that mark them as unique, and most don't want to.

I am no longer a working biologist, and as I've grown older, what most intrigues me about the natural world is the realization that there are all these lives out there, just beyond the four walls of my house, all these living, breathing creatures with beating hearts and pulsing blood, and eyes that see and ears that hear. They are all Out There, perceiving this world differently from the way I do, and well equipped to stay safe in it, mate, and raise offspring—unless our technological society gets in their way. The fact that they are not always visible just enhances the intrigue. The world is infinitely more complex than we can comprehend.

So the death of one, of ten, of hundreds by an automobile is tragic, because to those creatures, it matters. And because birds, mammals, and even reptiles are often social, the arc of impact is wide.

It's October, and the community around Pioneer Lake is getting restless. Daylight is quickly waning and the temps are cooling. It seems we should be off to somewhere, but only some of us have a destination in mind. The leopard frogs know where they're going. They're headed to the mucky bottoms of lakes and ponds where they will immerse themselves for the winter. Each fall, we have to contend with their mass migration. Nocturnal by inclination, they will cover the roads nearest the lakes each night, all hopping in one direction, drawn to the water. Driving home from choir practice last week, we saw the frogs appearing in our headlights as if riding miniature pogo sticks. Leopard frogs are astonishingly good hoppers. They can lift themselves three feet into the air—a remarkable feat for the possessor of such small muscles. Imagine a human high jumper having similar capabilities! We have a number of frogs in our yard—American toads, wood frogs, and gray tree frogs are very common—but none equals the leopard in agility.

Unfortunately, their acrobatics are no match for the automobile. A hop on the highway is a suicidal move. That is not to say that drivers at this time of year don't swerve, sideswipe, and brake for frogs. We do. The slow sashay of taillights down a country road is not an uncommon sight. But often the hoppers don't move until we're right up next to them, or they move unpredictably, or they are mistaken for a scuttling leaf—until too late. In the morning, we see the carnage: hundreds of flattened frog bodies drying on the pavement in the rising sun. I wonder what percentage of the migrators makes it safely to Pioneer Lake.

It has not always been this way. Paved roads and automobiles motoring about at night have been in Chisago County only about ninety years. Before then, we might assume that the ancestors of our leopard frogs hopped unmolested on fall nights toward the water and its protection from the winter. As I make my way home in the evening, I often think of how alive the earth once was.

I walked to church yesterday. It had rained all night, and in the gray light of Sunday morning the woods, yards, and fields were sodden, leaves limp with moisture. Oasis Road, running between our house and the church had been freshly paved a few days before. Out for a run on its black, unblemished surface only hours after it was laid down, I had marveled at its purity. It had been given a new beginning.

But walking to church, I could see the ebony surface had become a blackboard on which carnage was tallied. The rain had brought out the frogs, which now were migrating to the lake. Many frogs spend the summer in grassy meadows and woodlands, but most return to the water to overwinter. Thousands of frogs on the move had met with calamity. Pale, white bodies, or parts of bodies, were everywhere. An odor of fishy decay hung on the damp air.

I tried to avert my eyes, but it was hard not to see the tiny, splayed toes of a forelimb, flattened by a tire, or the long, slender hind legs, beautifully formed for prodigious jumping. One large leopard frog lay intact, so perfect that I admired its glossy moss-colored skin with its round dark polka-dots—until I saw the pink bubble of lungs and viscera extending out, underneath its throat.

Via Dolorosa, "the way of sorrow," the Christian Church calls it, the route Jesus took from judgment at Pilate's court to death at Golgotha. I walked my own little via dolorosa from my home to church.

# Saints at Work, Saints at Rest

Great horned owls disturbed my sleep on Halloween night. Their sonorous hoots, just outside my bedroom window, pulled me out of the deep tangled dreams of midnight. As I rose to the surface, slowly coming into consciousness, I mistook them for ghosts, and I wondered why unearthly spirits would want to visit me.

The alto section of the choir had been telling ghost stories that morning. We sat in the choir room after warm-up, dressed in our billowing green robes, and awaited the beginning of the festive Reformation Day service, commemorating Martin Luther's nailing of the ninety-five theses to the church door at Wittenberg. To pass the time, we discussed a recent article we'd seen in the Minneapolis *StarTribune*. Reporters had taken a psychic and visited several buildings in the area that seemed to have great potential for harboring ghosts. She had responded with sensations that could be traced to past figures that had once peopled the rooms. She felt a presence in each place; she could see forms and manner of dress with an "inner eye." With one ghost, she sensed a protective concern for a newspaper photographer also present in the room.

This interested the altos. None of us had ever seen a ghost, but we knew people who had. My aunt and uncle reportedly had haunted their former house for a while after their deaths. "But why," I wanted to know, "why aren't my peaceable relatives at rest?"

"Maybe they are. Maybe they liked their house," suggested one of the altos. This was true. They did like their house. My uncle, an architect, had designed it and they had lived in it for forty years. We thought about what it might mean to have ghosts in the world and fell silent. Then we went up to sing.

So ghosts were on my mind on Halloween night as the owls called outside my window, and the cries were not eerie but sweet, in a major key. Happy shades. Even so, while still asleep, I thought it would be unwise to open the window to ghosts. Then I came to wakefulness, recognized them as owls, probably those who nest in the woods at nearby Hillside Cemetery, and rose to lift the window.

The thicket outside was lit with moonlight. Though waning, there was enough moon to brighten the night and cast shadows. The owls, one pitched low, a bass, and the other higher, an alto, continued calling for a quarter of an hour. I lay in bed, washed in the cold air of November, held in their spell. I had no need of otherworldly visitors. Lulled by their melody, I fell back asleep.

I awoke to All Saints' Day.

Who are the saints? The Roman Catholic Church confers sainthood upon a small number of people who have performed distinctive acts, but my personal definition is broader and more democratic. Protestants consider all believers, living and dead, to be saints.

Saints can be hidden under various guises. Recently, one of our Audubon members died, in old age and after a long illness. Valeta was one of the first people I met when I joined our chapter twenty years ago. It was hard to overlook her. She'd sit in the front row during our monthly meetings and in a low, gravelly voice pepper the speaker with alert questions on any topic under discussion. She always had an interesting bird story to relate—an unusual number of cardinals coming to her feeder, or a Tennessee warbler dining on suet in May. It didn't matter to her whether the bird was common or uncommon; she appreciated the delicacy and loveliness of all winged creatures.

She had been a sixth grade teacher most of her life, introducing a new crop of children each year to the wonders of the natural world. She was interested in nearly all aspects of it, from little brown bats and wild flowers to monarch butterflies and edible mushrooms. Some of our chapter members had stayed at her rustic log cabin on the north shore of Lake Superior, a summer retreat lacking electricity and running water, but offering expansive views of the shimmering lake.

In the last weeks of her life, her sons had taken her to see the great lake one last time, much like the Ojibwe people have done for their elders. On the way home, they had happened upon a broad expanse of showy lady slippers, growing along a little-traveled road. I think the family took it as a beneficent sign. All in all, Valeta led a modest life, but one dedicated to witnessing the beauty of creation. When she died, she asked her sons to continue that witness at her wake and funeral.

Her first request was that bouquets of flowers sent in her memory be from the field, not the greenhouse. It was not an easy request to fulfill—consider all the bouquets that adorn a funeral and now imagine them composed only of blooms collected from roadsides and meadows. The local florists rose to the occasion, however, and when I entered the funeral chapel, a riot of bright, undisciplined wildflowers greeted me: asters and daisies, wood lilies and sweet clover. There was an entire arrangement made solely of white campion. Audubon members, recalling tromps in the woods with Valeta when she was young and hale, moved from one bouquet to the next as if on a field trip (Valeta would have loved it), identifying each species in turn. In one corner of the room, her sons had arranged a display of her dearest books. There were well-worn field guides to North American birds and Minnesota wild flowers. There was a how-to guide, *Woodworking for Wildlife*. There was the complete collection of Sigurd Olson's books on the North Country, all in hardcover, old and well thumbed.

Valeta herself was laid out in a red-and-black buffalo plaid–lined coffin. She was dressed in a sweatshirt that had a loon on the front. On the lower end of the casket sat a display featuring native woodland ferns and a piece of bracken fungus. I don't believe I had ever commemorated the passing of a human being along with so many other members of creation. It brought to mind a verse of a familiar hymn that seemed fitting for a funeral:

> To all, life Thou givest, to both great and small;
> In all life Thou livest, the true life of all.
> We blossom and flourish like leaves on a tree,
> And wither and perish, but naught changeth thee.

Valeta's funeral led me to contemplate my own. In what manner would I like to pass from the scene? Anyone who loves nature has some idea of a fitting, natural end to life. A walk in the woods reveals a mound of feathers where once was a bird, or a mat of coarse fur, a former raccoon. Once while cross-country skiing in a spruce bog on a cold, crystalline day, I happened upon a deer skeleton with each bone in place but not one piece of skin or flesh remaining—such had been the feast that deer had provided. A natural death is generous. Every part becomes food for something else.

Year in, year out, I watch my garden compost pile with great interest. It is wonderful how grapefruit rinds, potato peels, cornhusks, and apple cores transform into dark, rich soil that enhances my garden beds. The earth works this miracle right outside my kitchen window little by little, each day.

For people who entertain visions of being returned to the earth, it is not so easy, especially in the United States. Bodies are almost always embalmed with formaldehyde, a compound that draws the water out of the cells to preserve them and greatly retard decomposition, much like brine does to cucumbers. These pickled bodies are then placed in sealed, hardwood coffins that are secured, in turn, in concrete burial vaults. The return of bodily remains to the earth, as in a compost pile, is not possible. Our local funeral director told me firmly that everybody gets a burial vault.

It doesn't have to be this way.

A fellow Auduboner gave me an article on "Green Graveyards" a few weeks ago. It described a woodland graveyard in South Carolina called Ramsey Canyon Preserve. Begun by a local doctor who is also an environmentalist, the unconventional cemetery receives nonembalmed bodies in biodegradable caskets, or merely in shrouds, and marks the graves with simple, flat, engraved stones. The cemetery preserve is laced with hiking trails, a pleasant place to hike or picnic. All of this is up to South Carolina code—but it is unique. And few other places in the country emulate it.

Elsewhere in the world, people have other options. In Great Britain, environmentalists ask questions one never hears raised in the United States: What does the presence of formaldehyde in a body do to the groundwater? What is the impact on hardwood forests in using cherry, oak, and maple caskets? How much greenhouse gas is produced to rev up a crematorium to turn a body to ash at high temperatures? Web sites in the United Kingdom direct people to burial parks for those who would like to be buried in natural settings, which would also provide habitat for birds and other wildlife. There's even a Green Endings site, where people can enlist the services of a funeral planner, much like a wedding coordinator, to get the details right on an environmentally conscious burial. You don't want to plunder the forest for fine wood that will only be sunk in the earth? Log on and view the alternatives: wicker baskets, woolen shrouds, and something that looks like our car top cargo carrier.

In this country, we are a long way from these enlightened practices. My local funeral director told me no one had ever talked to him about a "green funeral" before. With all the environmental crises in the land of the living these days, I'm not inclined to tilt at windmills in the land of the dead. Though I would heed the poet, Dylan Thomas, and "not go gentle into that good night," once I'm gone, I'd like to be sent off with a minimum of fuss and as little impact as possible.

On the southeast end of Pioneer Lake, the saints of the yellow brick church rest in Hillside Cemetery. We sang in praise of their faithful lives last Sunday, All Saints' Sunday, in a service marked by flickering flames and white linen swathing the altar. Amid the candles bright with fire, I, as reader for the day, named them: "These are they who have come out of the great ordeal," a passage from the book of Revelation.

In the cemetery, the lawn has become tawny with the aging of the fall. The sugar maples stand bereft of leaves and a chilly northwest wind comes off the lake. November is an austere month, when the bones of the land are laid bare. I walk among the headstones and mull over the reading from Revelation. The phrase "the great ordeal" resonates with me. Life sometimes seems like an ordeal. I think most people feel this way at some point in their lives. I have not yet personally experienced the ravages of disease or death. My life has been exceptionally felicitous, but in my wider existence as a member of creation, there seems an unrelenting downward spiral into destruction and disintegration of nature.

When my Audubon magazine arrived in the mail last month, it featured a pullout section on the state of birds. North American birds are not doing well. Twenty-three percent of all species—nearly one quarter of North American birds—are at risk of extinction because of declining populations. Two species are ordinary ones that until very recently I saw daily around Pioneer Lake: common nighthawks and pine siskins.

Nighthawks used to display around the steeple of the church in spring and summer. In fall, we'd see impressive spirals of hundreds of birds as they swirled high over our heads, preparing to migrate. No nighthawks this year on Pioneer. The article said their population has been reduced to half of what it was.

Pine siskins are modest, streaked birds that congregate with their cousins, American goldfinches, at backyard feeders. They ought to be part of the usual mix of winter birds. No pine siskins at my feeder these days. Their numbers, too, have been cut in half.

"These are they who have come out of the Great Ordeal," I think to myself, tracing my way back and forth through the rows of granite. I imagine what lies ahead: witnessing the last wild panda in China, the last Florida panther in the Everglades, the last polar bear. Even Jane Goodall's chimps are in trouble.

"These are they who have come out of the Great Ordeal." Everyone can point to their own imagination of a great ordeal: genocide, mass starvation, war. Maybe it is more personal, such as a drawn-out death from cancer or the inarticulate life of a stroke victim. The environmentalist version takes shape as we count our losses, as the earth's creatures that Saint Francis called "our brothers and sisters" wink out, one by one.

We who reside on the eastern shore of Pioneer know something about death, loss, and grief, perhaps more than others since we live each day with Hillside Cemetery. We know the process, at least, of how we commit our saints to the earth. Sometimes I see Dale, keeper of the cemetery books and purveyor of the plots, out walking with someone among the markers, looking for a gravesite. Sometimes I am passing by as the earthmover is digging out a grave, piling the soil high in mounds beside the hole. Mornings, afternoons, I might be witness to how the local undertakers attempt to soften the bald fact of dirt and holes with fake grass carpet covering the mound and a civilized canopy erected to shelter the mourners—as if a mortal blow comes from an open sky and not from deep within us.

Then there are the gatherings. Driving by on my way to the grocery store or to the high school, I will see a knot of dark, somber figures, a white-robed pastor with a Bible, the hearse in the background. Grief is palpable.

But most of the visits to Hillside are solitary. Year in, year out, this is what I see: a wife who sits by her husband's grave, gazing out over the lake; a grieving young woman who for months lights an evening candle on the grave of her best friend; the flickering taillights of an automobile visiting the snowy cemetery at midnight after the Christmas Eve service.

Hillside Cemetery and cemeteries everywhere are not expressly for the saints at rest but for the saints still laboring. They are havens for people who strive every day to care for children, do a good job, be true to the faith, shore up a disintegrating world, secure a future for all the earth's creatures. They offer a space in which to sit and be quiet, space in which to try to figure it all out. I have been witness to healing in cemeteries.

That is why I have rejected the notion of having my ashes, when I die, scattered to the winds. I want my remains collected in one place, so that there is one specific spot for my loved ones to come and gather their thoughts. I want the cemetery owls to hoot in a major key over my grave. And I want to lie with the saints, my friends and neighbors in life. We'll all be here together, finally at rest.

# Everyone a King

One last paddle in the canoe on Pioneer before ice-over. As I pick my way past yellowing vegetation lining the path to the lake, I can see that the color has drained from the land in the past fortnight. The brilliant maples in our side yard have dropped their leaves. The ruby oaks have browned. Farmers have been at work in the fields surrounding the marshy basin. They've shorn the apricot-colored soybeans and reduced the corn to stubble. The contours of the earth stand revealed, like the subtle topography of a skull.

The growing season, which began in April, has closed. I have only carrots remaining in my garden; the chilly soil preserves them well. The lake's aquatic ecosystem also responds to the coming winter. Its water has cleared as the algal population declines under the assault of colder and colder temperatures. Once more, I can see the silty bottom, littered with fallen box elder leaves, as I peer into the water from the shore.

We took the dock in last weekend. The sheltie, startled to see Tom rigged up in the oafish attire of waders, stood at the water's edge and barked herself hoarse from alarm. We had not been on the water in weeks, and the dock will not be missed until next spring. Without the domesticity of a pier, Pioneer's shoreline has reverted to a wild state. It feels like I am farther north, closer to wilderness, as I maneuver the canoe off its rack and ease its silky hull into the water. I swing it around so that the gunwale is parallel to the water's edge, step carefully in, placing my foot at the midline to keep it upright, and ease into a kneeling position, so I can paddle the craft from its middle. I admire the water's clarity as I head out toward deeper water. If only Pioneer could always appear this pristine.

The past Sunday was Christ the King Sunday, the last Sunday of the church year. The music for this lesser festival of the church tends to be expansive and grand. "Christ is the King! O Friends, rejoice; Brothers and sisters with one voice," the choir sings as we process slowly up the aisle with as much pomp as a rural Lutheran congregation can muster. Lutheran roots extend deep into Scandinavia and Germany, but in the New World, the music is heavily influenced by the denomination sharing the common tongue: the Anglicans. The Church of England, entwined as it is with political empire, a monarch at its head, has honed its expression of a kingly presence to a fine art. There are trumpets with fanfares, a cacophonous pipe organ, brocade and banners, and dignified postures.

I find this fun most times and even diverting, but each year while we amuse ourselves with lordly kings, the true Christ, the one who entered the world in a shabby manner and exited it in a painful and ignoble death, fades from sight, like the hues from the November countryside. We often hear exhortations to be modest servants, but such figures don't process down a church aisle. Maybe servants can only be seen with peripheral vision, while the central focus is on a lordly distraction.

It is a somber morning on the water. I dip into the pellucid lake at regular intervals and listen to the drip of liquid running down the paddle's blade. The brisk air numbs my exposed skin. I wear gloves and a winter hat. In keeping with the revelatory nature of November, I can see more clearly the features of Pioneer's shoreline now that the leaves are down. Each yard extending outward from its house bears the mark of the homeowner's distinctive treatment.

I have been confounded by the fact that people can truly own a parcel of land and that they can do with it as they please. This bafflement has put me at odds with our so-called "ownership society," where money is the ultimate power broker. I find myself tongue-tied in discussions of property rights, when landowners complain that legislation crafted to protect endangered species, for example, devalues their investment. There are no words in our American lingo that can trump the language of money.

Far from shore, in the center of the lake, I am forcefully confronted with the evidence that I am out of step. Nearly every lakeshore owner has wielded their property rights with vigor. Some have cleared away the understory of the remnant forest that recently grew along the water, presumably so they could see the water from the house. Others, not many, have removed all native vegetation and replaced it with an open lawn that sweeps directly to the Pioneer's edge. One owner, a tidy and exacting gardener, has crafted steps and formal plantings all the way down his hill.

On the other hand, some have only run a single path through the tangle of brush and canopy trees so that, from my perspective on the water, it seems a perfectly intact patch of woods. This is misleading—I know that our hands-off approach allows the aggressive nonnative buckthorn to flourish and suppress shrubs that would be more beneficial to wildlife. Still others, only two, mercifully, have wiped out every woody plant from the hillside and terraced it with introduced fieldstone. The result is a brutally exposed and barren hillside. These two yards on the western shore bear the heaviest human imprint on Pioneer.

The book of Genesis contains the account of the Fall, the story in which the first people, Adam and Eve, beguiled by a serpent, disobey God and eat fruit from a forbidden tree. The act results in estrangement between the Creator and the created, who subsequently toil in producing food and are banished from their first home, a beneficent garden. Sin begins with the first bite of the apple.

I have loved this story since childhood, and it has grown both in meaning and mystery to me over the years. All my life I have wondered why humans cannot live peaceably with the rest of creation. Since becoming a biologist, I have acquired more sophisticated means of pondering the tale. There seems to be some hard nut of truth in Genesis. It is a very old book, and the story of the Fall tells me that a perceptive writer, thousands of years ago, also intuited that something was fundamentally amiss in our relationship with nature. This mismatch is not merely due to our twenty-first century advanced technology.

"It doesn't seem to be here that we belong, here where space is curved, the earth is round, we're all going to die, and it seems as wise to stay in bed as budge," observes Annie Dillard. "It is strange here, not quite warm enough, or too warm, too leafy or inedible, or windy, or dead. It is not frankly, the sort of home for people one would have thought of." When I was a child, a favorite hymn of our congregation went, "I'm but a stranger here, Heaven is my home. Earth is a desert drear, heaven is my home." Even when young, I recoiled while singing this. I loved the earth. As an adult, I am extremely uncomfortable with the mixed message

Christianity seems to send about our place in the natural world. Why does the story of the Fall resonate so vibrantly?

At times I have wondered exactly what, in terms I can understand, this original sin is. Many of the "sins" so rife in the human race merely derive from being an animal. Selfishness? We're just maximizing our own chances of surviving and reproducing. Greed? Likewise. Adultery? It's one way of getting as many of our genes into the next generation as possible. Sloth? Animals never waste calories extending themselves beyond what they have to do.

Is it a sin, then, to be an animal?

What an absurd idea, that animals are sinful. At the heart of sin is an understanding that we willfully choose a wrong course of action or reject a right one. Surely at the crux of original sin is the idea of free will. Perhaps, then, Eve bit into that apple during the course of our evolution of consciousness. Consciousness: that little voice keeping up a running patter inside our head, the unending internal monologue that says, "No, no, you shouldn't be doing this!" or "Yes, of course, that's the right thing to do," and also, "Go ahead—just do it. No one will ever know."

This explanation would be more satisfactory if I could be sure that only humans possess consciousness. But it is quite possible we share the quality of self-awareness with at least our closest kin, the other great apes: chimpanzees and gorillas. Their demonstrated rudimentary command of language hints at the existence of an inner life. And then there are dolphins, with their complex language and social system, highly intelligent and curious. What might be going on inside their bottle-nosed heads?

Researchers have long been interested in the question of animal awareness, but it is a tricky topic to investigate, made perhaps insurmountably difficult by the impossibility of penetrating a different species' thoughts. We have problems understanding our own thoughts! How can we know what a dog mulls over?

Nevertheless, even just among the mammals, we share the well-developed cerebral cortex. Cat and dog owners know that something goes on behind those round eyes—they are not little automatons. This human estrangement from nature cannot be due to the fact that we think and the rest of creation does not.

Far from shore, in the middle of Pioneer, where the water-ski course was anchored all summer, I peer into the dark water. The sky is overcast and a breeze ruffles the surface. Although the water column has cleared, I can still see no farther than two feet down. Beneath, the dark murk is a stark contrast to the open, available shoreline.

I stop paddling and let the canoe rock on the waves. They come rolling out of the northwest, out from the edge of the wild alder thicket, to knock rhythmically against the length of the boat. The sound of their lap momentarily brings back the summer. July—when it was sunny and life seemed so straightforward. The canoe swings around, and off on the port side the great, simple form of the church comes into view. The steeple has clean, elegant lines. Nothing superfluous clutters its rise.

Perhaps I am reading too much into Genesis. The writer records God's observation that "the man has become one of us." The heart of the sin is the desire to be godlike. What does this mean? A thrust for power, for dominion? The desire for complete knowledge, and the hubris to think that we can, given enough time and study, achieve it? I think this is nearer the truth than proposals that cultural or biological markers initiated the rift—like the rise of agriculture, or the evolution of consciousness.

I'll take it one step further and suggest that the original sin lies in what kind of god we chose to be. All the major environmental crises of this century—global warming, ozone layer destruction, deforestation, to name but a few—derive from an exercise of power over nature. It is a power akin to that of a plundering monarch who seeks to control, exploit, and subjugate the rest of creation. It is the kind of king that reigns over an empire, bending each component to his will, to his own ends.

What if, instead, we chose to emulate the kind of king Christians believe Jesus to be—a servant who heals, tends, and waits on others, one who suffers with us? What, then, would our relationship to nature be like?

From my vantage point in the canoe floating without anchor in the November wind, I study the parcels of land that people own around the lake. Which ones belong to plunderers and which to servants? How has Pioneer flourished under human influence? How have we waited upon the needs of the natural community?

Pioneer is fed by a natural spring, so that fresh water is continually bubbling up into the lake from the underlying water table. But far more water rolls off the surrounding banks—the watershed—than enters from the spring. For the lake to thrive, that runoff needs to be clean and pure. But rain that falls on paved roads picks up dust, oil, and gasoline residue. In order to cleanse the water running into Pioneer from the roads that surround it, the soil and plants on its banks should be healthy and functional.

Landowners who have retained trees, shrubs, and small plants on their plot serve the lake well. The few who have not—notably the naked, stone-terraced hillside crafters—

have treated Pioneer as if it were a thing, a bathtub, if you will, that has no relationship to what surrounds it; it becomes filled with foul water. The hillside terracers have sinned—if you will grant me that it is a sin—out of ignorance, surely. We do not teach about watersheds in our high school biology classes. How would people get that knowledge?

"We have sinned against you in thought, word and deed, by what we have done and by what we have left undone," the confession reads, at the start of a worship service. The estrangement from nature is in part merely one of not knowing, and of having so many people not knowing, that their collective actions harm the rest of creation. Servants allow their masters to be fully themselves by careful observation of their habits. Thus, servanthood involves study and observation, a solid base of knowledge, so that the needs are more fully known.

Another deadly contaminant to enter Pioneer is the element phosphorus. Phosphorus, in the form of phosphate, naturally occurs in plants and acts as a fertilizer promoting growth if plants lack optimal amounts. It was once a dominant component of lawn fertilizer, but it has been so lavishly applied over the years that the world is now awash with phosphorus. We recently submitted a soil sample from our garden to be analyzed and were surprised to learn it measured off the charts in phosphorus content, even though we in our thirteen years here have never applied phosphorus fertilizer. We wonder if that phosphorus might derive from the 1920s and 1930s, when our yard was a garden plot for a family living in town.

In the biosphere, most of the phosphorus is still sequestered in phosphate-containing rocks, and in one of the oddities of nature, in guano deposits of seabirds. Since the onset of large-scale mining operations to produce phosphate-containing fertilizer, however, a huge supply of phosphorus has been taken out of sequestration and made available to the living world in immense quantities, upsetting a delicate balance between different species of plants.

Pioneer becomes less than fully functional as phosphorus pours into its waters. Blue-green algae thrive under high levels, and their burgeoning populations outcompete other types of algae that form the basis of the aquatic food chain. Servants aid Pioneer in self-realization by eschewing phosphates and maintaining buffer strips of vegetation along the shore that take up the excess element before it reaches the water.

Ecologist Aldo Leopold, groping toward an ethical framework that is based on ecological relationship, wrote sixty years ago that ecology could determine right from wrong: "A thing is right when it tends to preserve the integrity, stability and beauty of the biotic community. It is wrong when it tends otherwise." I cannot argue against that. But what I see, sitting in the canoe under the chill of a northwest wind, is the need for something far less lofty, more simple, more basic: the need to simply "love your neighbor as yourself."

And who is our neighbor? This is the question people put to Jesus in the Gospel accounts, hoping perhaps to be freed from having to love unsavory types, those displaying different ethnicities or values perhaps. In the Bible, the neighbor, though, is always a human being.

However, I tend to a broad interpretation. My neighbors on Pioneer include all who share the oxygen I breathe, the water I drink, the soil I'm rooted in. The red foxes who ran past my window on Valentine's Day, the otters who left their belly prints in the snow, the goose with the broken wing, the winking fireflies, the hundreds of migrating leopard frogs—all of these are my neighbors. Even the beleaguered little lake upon which I float in my canoe at this moment is my neighbor, and I am commanded to love it. I am urged to wait upon my neighbors and to suffer with them.

It is late afternoon and the overcast day is losing light. Sunset comes early in late November. It is time to head in toward the brightness and warmth of the house, to start supper, to gather the family. My fingers have stiffened with the cold.

I pick up my paddle, execute a broad sweep, and turn the canoe into the wind. A pair of mallards, lingering late in the season, is coming in for a landing. They settle on to the water and adjust their feathers, to snuggle in for the night and to await the coming day.

**Sue Leaf** is a freelance writer and the author of *Potato City: History, Nature, and Community in the Age of Sprawl.* Her essays have appeared in *Minnesota Monthly, Utne Reader, Minnesota Conservation Volunteer,* and *Architecture Minnesota.* A former college instructor in biology and environmental science, she holds a doctorate in zoology from the University of Minnesota. She is president of Wild River Audubon and lives in Center City, Minnesota, on the shore of Pioneer Lake.